The Usatges of Barcelona

University of Pennsylvania Press
MIDDLE AGES SERIES
Edited by
Edward Peters
Henry Charles Lea Professor
of Medieval History
University of Pennsylvania

A listing of the available books
in the series appears at the
back of this volume

The Usatges of Barcelona

The Fundamental Law of Catalonia

Translated, with an introduction
and notes, by Donald J. Kagay

University of Pennsylvania Press

Philadelphia

Copyright © 1994 by the University of Pennsylvania Press
Printed in the United States of America

Library of Congress Cataloging-in-Publication Data
The Usatges of Barcelona : the fundamental law of Catalonia / translated and with an
introduction by Donald J. Kagay.
    p.   cm. — (Middle Ages series)
    Includes bibliographical references and index.
    ISBN 0-8122-3256-9 (cloth). — ISBN 0-8122-1535-4 (pbk.)
    1. Law — Spain — Catalonia — Sources.   2. Law — Spain — Catalonia — History.
3. Usatges de Barcelona. Catalan & Latin. I. Kagay, Donald J. II. Usatges de Barcelona.
Catalan & Latin. III. Series.
KKT6071.A178U83 1994
349.46'7 — dc20
[344.67]   94-28919
                                                CIP

Contents

Preface

In the second part of his great novel, Cervantes has the Knight of Sad Countenance enter a printing shop of Barcelona and utter the following words:

> it seems to me that translating from one language into another . . . is like viewing Flemish tapestries on the wrong side; for, although you see the pictures, they are covered with threads which obscure them so the smoothness and gloss of the fabric is lost. (Miguel de Cervantes, *The Adventures of Don Quijote*, ed. J. M. Cohen [1950; reprint New York: Penguin Books, 1983], part II, chap. 62, p. 877)

Such is the bane of any translator. How can one retain the "figures" of the original text while transmitting it into one's own language? This quandary is further complicated when the text in question is over seven hundred years old; not only must its words be translated but the obsolete societal usages they describe must also be made clear. To remain within these margins, I have followed the Bastardas i Parera Latin edition as closely as modern usage allows. In the majority of the *Usatges* articles, as in many modern law codes, a form of judicial syllogism uses the first clause to outline a certain situation and proceeds, and the second to state the law's response to it. With few exceptions, the authors of the code used future more vivid conditional with the future perfect indicative to form such clauses. At times, they lapse into the present subjunctive for the second part of the syllogism. In both forms, the phrase is best translated in the English present indicative. Nouns and adjectives follow classical norms more closely but even with these forms a large number of neologisms have entered the code in Latin raiment. The most important of these are treated in text footnotes.

It is thus hoped that the translation here may be rendered faithfully in accordance with the idiosyncrasies of the original and in line with the rules of modern English. If I prove successful at this task, the assessment of translation by the Knight of the Sad Countenance must convey some dubious satisfaction:

> But I do not mean to imply that this exercise of translation is not praiseworthy; for, a man might be occupied in worse things and less profitable occupations. (877)

Abbreviations

Frequently cited works will be abbreviated in the following manner:

ACA   Archivo de la Corona de Aragón, Barcelona

Anuari   *Anuari de l'Institut d'Estudis Catalans*

AEM   *Anuario de Estudios Medievales*

AHDE   *Anuario de Historia del derecho español*

AHR   *American Historical Review*

BRABLB   *Boletin de Real Academia de Buenas Letras de Barcelona*

BRAH   *Boletin de Real Academia de Historia*

CAVC   *Colección de las Cortes de los antiguos reinos de Aragón y de Valencia y el principado de Cataluña.* Edited by Fidel Fita y Colomé and Bienvenido Oliver y Esteller. 27 vols. Madrid: Real Academia de Historia, 1806–1922.

CDACA   *Colección de documentos inéditos del Archivo General de la Corona de Aragón.* Edited by Prospero Bofarull y Moscaró. 42 vols. Barcelona: J. Eusebio Montfort, 1850–56.

CHCA   *Congreso de historia de la Corona de Aragón.* Congress number precedes title

CHE   *Cuadernos de Historia de España*

CSCV   *Cartulario de "Sant Cugat" de Valles.* Edited by José Rius Serra. 3 vols. Barcelona: Sobs. de López Robert et al., 1945–47.

CSJP   *The Chronicle of San Juan de la Peña: A Fourteenth-Century Official History of the Crown of Aragon.* Edited by Lynn Nelson. Philadelphia: University of Pennslyvania Press, 1991

DJ   *Documentos de Jaime I.* Edited by Ambrosio Huici Miranda and Maria Desamperados Cabanes Pecourt. 4 vols. Valencia: Anubar, 1976–82

DMA   *Dictionary of the Middle Ages.* Edited by Joseph R. Strayer et al. 13 vols. New York: Scribners, 1982–89

EG   *La formació i expansió del feudalisme català*. Edited by Jaume
                Portella i Comas. Actes del Col.loqui Organisat per Col.legi
                Universitari de Girona, 8–11 de Gener de 1985: Homenatge
                a Santiago Sobreques i Vidal *Estudi General* 5–6. Gerona:
                Col.legi Universitari de Girona, 1985–86.

EUC   *Estudis Universitaris Catalans*

GCB   *Gesta comitum barchinonensium. Textos llatí i català*. Edited
                by Louis Barrau-Dihigo and Jaume Massó Torrents. *Cròni-
                ques catalanes*, 2. Barcelona: Institut d'Estudis Catalans,
                1925

HC   *Historia de Catalunya: Biografiés Catalans*. Reprint series,
                Editorial Vicens Vives, 1979–81.

Handbuch   *Mittelalter. Die Geleheten Rechte und die Gesetzgebung*. Vol. 1
                of *Handbuch der Quellen und Literatur der Neuren Euro-
                päischen Privatrechts Geschichte*. Edited by Helmut Coing. 3
                vols. in 7 pts. Munich: 1973–88

LFM   *Liber Feudorum Maior*. Edited by Francisco Miguel Rosell. 2
                vols. Barcelona: Consejo Superior de Investigaciónes Cien-
                tíficas. Sección de Estudios Medievales de Barcelona, 1945–
                47

LV   *Leges Visigothorum. Monumenta Germaniae Historica.
                Legum: sectio I*. Edited by Karl Zeumer. Hanover: Hahn,
                1902

Marca   *Marca hispanica sive limes hispanicus, hoc est, geographica et
                historica Cataloniae, Ruscinonis, et circumiacentium popu-
                lorum*. Compiled by Pierre de Marca; Edited by Étienne
                Baluze. Paris: F. Maguet, 1688. Reprint. Barcelona: Edi-
                torial Base, 1972

MRAH   *Memorias de la Real Academia de Historia*

RABM   *Revista de Archivos, Bibliotecas, y Museos*

Structures   *Structures féodales et féodalisme dans l'Occident méditerranéen,
féodales   Xe–XIIIe siècles: Bilan et perspectives de recherches*. Colloque
                International organisé par la Centre National de la Re-
                cherche Scientifique et l'École Française de Rome, Rome,
                10–13 October 1978. Rome: École Française de Rome, 1983

Introduction

The Importance of the *Usatges of Barcelona*

Law is a systematic force that humans create in order to regulate both public and private social relations. One may be said to "possess" a law if the applicability of the law depends on individual status or membership in a particular society; one may be said to be "subject to" a law if the applicability of the law is universal throughout a specific territory. The difference betweeen "personal" and "territorial" law characterizes much of late antique and medieval legal and social history.

From the fifth century of the Common Era, territorial law of the Roman Empire was replaced in many of the new Germanic kingdoms by the personal laws of the different groups that constituted these kingdoms.[1] Roman law itself became the "personal" law of provincial Romans. The personal character of the "folk laws" later changed to accommodate the newer "feudal" relations between lords and vassals.[2] From the twelfth century, the intricate and learned old territorial law of Rome was rediscovered. The study of the imperial codes began to undermine the older laws of personal status, the rules governing the relations between lord and vassal, and the essentially oral method of preserving and transmitting the older law. Kings and princes, served by men trained in the Italian or southern French centers of education in the Roman law, readily turned to the systematic and highly articulated jurisprudence of imperial Rome as a conceptual base that could be used to override or outflank older folk or feudal strictures.[3]

Under this influence, much of Europe shifted from "personal" legal

---

1. Simeon Leonard Guterman, *From Personal to Territorial Law* (Metuchen, NJ: Scarecrow Press, 1972), 1–31; Norman Zacour, *An Introduction to Medieval Institutions* (New York: St. Martin's Press, 1976), 122–27.
2. Guterman, *From Personal to Territorial Law*, 33–34.
3. Stephan Kuttner, "The Revival of Jurisprudence," *Renaissance and Renewal in the Twelfth Century*, ed. Robert L. Benson and Giles Constable (Cambridge, MA: Harvard University Press, 1982), 300–304, 318–22; Knut Wolfgang Nörr, "Institutional Foundations of the New Jurisprudence," *Renaissance and Renewal*, ed. Benson and Constable 324–29.

systems toward those with a territorial base. The rulers (whether holding a royal or some other princely title) governed "homelands" (*patriae*), and the laws they approved or enacted were valid as far as their power ran. Far from being displaced, however, feudal relations were now regularized and they eventually entered into the realm of written, learned law. No code of the twelfth century illustrates this complex process and relects more of the various legal forces of the era as does the *Usatges of Barcelona*.[4]

The significance of the Barcelona code can scarcely be overstated in local Catalan and general European terms. Issued in the mid-twelfth century by officials and judges within the court of Count Ramon Berenguer IV of Barcelona (1131–62), the laws effectively defined both Catalonia itself and the dynasty that would rule it for five centuries. This disparate collection of feudal practice, peace and truce statutes, and excerpts from Roman and Visigothic law codes became the source from which all other Catalan laws flowed. In reality, its hybrid nature may explain how the *Usatges* came to be Catalonia's fundamental law. As a composite of so many different legal elements, the code, or at least parts of it, gave something for almost everyone to claim. With the general acceptance of them in Catalonia, the laws began to influence legal forms in neighboring southern France and in realms of the Crown of Aragon. In time, they came to symbolize a Catalan nationalism long suppressed but not defeated by Castile.

The *Usatges* were also highly significant in regard to contemporaneous European legal trends. The code serves as a juridical litmus test that can measure with some accuracy the transmission of learned Roman law from Italy or southern France into Catalonia.[5] It also shows how important the experience of rediscovered Roman law was to both royal administration and the renewal of legislation within Catalonia and throughout Europe.[6] The creators of the *Usatges* were not simply scribes but were in a sense scholars who used new trends in learned law to rectify the judicial norms of

---

4. Charles Homer Haskins, *The Renaissance of the Twelfth Century* (New York: Houghton Mifflin, 1912; New York: New American Library, 1972), 197–99; Georges Duby, *The Chivalrous Society*, trans. Cynthia Postan (Berkeley: University of California Press, 1977; reprint. 1980), 56–58.

5. Guillermo Maria de Broca y Montagut, *Historia del derecho de Cataluña, especialmente de civil* (Barcelona: Herederos de Juan Gili, 1918; Barcelona: Generalitat de Castalunya, Departament de Justícia, 1988), 179–81.

6. Jean-Pierre Poly and Eric Bournazel, *The Feudal Transformation, 900–1200*, trans. Caroline Higgitt (1980; reprint, New York: Holmes and Meier, 1991), 202–4; Kuttner, "Revival of Jurisprudence," *Renaissance and Renewal*, ed. Benson and Constable, 305; Nörr "Institutional Foundations," *Renaissance and Renewal*, ed. Benson ans Constable, 326–29; Armin Wolf, "Gesetzgebung und Kodifikationen," *Die Renaissance der Wissenschaften im 12. Jahrhundert*, ed. Peter Weimar (Zurich: Artemis, 1981), 144–45, 148–49.

their own land. When the learned law seemed to fail, they used its "style" to address new situations. If the local customary law was silent on a certain point, they simply fabricated novel and learned elements. In the case of the *Usatges*, they even occasionally acted as forgers on a grand scale, attributing their work to the court of Ramón Berenguer I of the mid-eleventh century. Yet, as Michael Clanchy has pointed out, such legal counterfeiters were indeed "experts at the center of the literary and intellectual culture" of the era.[7] Their work, then, was not simply a transformation of customary feudal practice into writing, nor was it a true statutory law, since the sovereigns who commissioned it are not even mentioned in it. Like many other codes of the twelfth century, the *Usatges* comprised a set of academic laws which represented the feudal world not exactly as it was but as the "law givers" (*legislatores*) professed to see it.

The Emergence of Barcelona and Catalonia: A Maze Among Iberian Mazes

Spain was born in a violent geological past in which one range of mountains after another was thrown up across the countryside. As a result, the Iberian Peninsula entered history as one of Europe's most mountainous regions.[8] Nowhere has this mountainous aspect more touched the affairs of *homo ibericus* than in the northeastern corner of the Peninsula known as Catalonia. In geological and geographical terms, Catalonia is a microcosm of Iberia itself. Ringed by cordilleras of various ages and heights, the land is itself divided by mountain ranges into three distinct zones. To the north, Catalonia is separated from and linked to France by the Pyrenees.[9] The Pyrenean passes formed thoroughfares between Spain and France long before either existed as states. The route of the *Via Domitia*, which connected Perpignan to Barcelona, led down into Catalonia's second geo-

---

7. Michael T. Clanchy, *From Memory to Written Record, 1066–1301* (Cambridge, MA: Harvard University Press, 1979), 249.

8. James Macintosh Houston, *The Western Mediterranean World: An Introduction to Its Regional Landscapes* (London: Longman, 1964; New York: Praeger, 1967), 186–87; Donald J. Kagay, "Catalonia," *Historical Dictionary of Modern Spain, 1700–1988*, ed. Robert W. Kern (New York: Greenwood Press, 1988), 125.

9. Norman J. G. Pounds, *An Historical Geography of Europe 450 B.C.–A.D. 1330* (Cambridge: Cambridge University Press, 1973), 2, 5; Clifford Thorpe Smith, *An Historical Geography of Western Europe Before 1800* (New York: Praeger, 1967), 171, 246; Peregrine Hordern and Nicholas Purcell, *The Mediterranean World: Man and Environment in Antiquity and the Middle Ages* (Oxford: Oxford University Press, 1987).

graphical zone, that of the Mediterranean littoral. For most of its length, this *costa brava* is as Richard Ford described it in 1845: "wild and picturesque."[10] The very irregularity of the coastline and lack of navigable inlets has bestowed a position of commercial dominance on Barcelona, the only large port in region.[11] By and large, these first two geographical zones constitute the region which came to be known as Old Catalonia. New Catalonia, the district conquered from Islam from the late eleventh century onward, forms the third. Bounded by the Segre River and the cities of Tarragona, Lerida, and Tortosa, this great wedge of fertile territory owes its existence more to riverine than to tectonic forces. As Catalonia's greatest river, the Ebro, meanders from its source in the Sierra del Cadi to its mouth below Tortosa, a great alluvial basin is deposited and constantly resculpted. This swath of flatland, broken only occasionally by escarpments, has long lent itself to large-scale irrigational agriculture.[12]

The political divisions of the land that would become Catalonia are clearly reflected from its geography. Thus it was no accident that Barcelona, the preeminent port of the region, came to dominate the Ebro *huerta* and eventually the Pyrenean uplands. Such a development, however, could only take place because of the remarkable drive of the counts of Barcelona as well as the fairly isolated geographical arena in which this expansion took place. From its physical nature as "a refuge and labyrinth," Catalonia was given its political character.[13]

The Triumph of Catalonia and the Count of Barcelona

Northeastern Spain has from prehistoric times served as a entrepot. Under the Roman Empire, the region comprised a large part of *Tarraconensis*, the most important of the Roman provinces carved out of the Iberian Penin-

10. Richard Ford, *A Hand-Book for Travellers in Spain and Readers at Home*, 3 vols. (London: Murray, 1845; reprint, Carbondale: Southern Illinois University Press, 1966), 2: 768.

11. Houston, *Western Mediterranean World*, 274–75; William Baynes Fisher and Howard Bowen-Jones, *Spain: An Introductory Geography* (London: Chatto and Windus, 1958; New York: Praeger, 1966), 99.

12. Houston, *Western Mediterranean World*, 189–90; Margaret Reid Shackleton, *Europe: A Regional Geography* (New York: Longman Green, 1934; New York: Praeger, 1964), 111–12; Fisher and Bowen-Jones, *Spain*, 156.

13. Pierre Vilar, *La Catalogne dans l'espagne moderne: Recherches sur les fondements économiques des structures nationales*, 3 vols. (Paris: S.E.V.P.E.N., 1962), 1: 198–99.

sula.[14] It retained its significance even after the Visigothic invasions of the fifth century. Despite the lingering importance of Tarragona as the province's metropolitan see, Barcelona emerged as the area's greatest administrative and commercial center. Even after the Visigothic ruling house shifted its power base to Toledo in the seventh century, Barcelona remained the most active port of the realm. Its clergy, though briefly falling under the spell of the Arian heresy in the late sixth century, formed a significant missionary force for the conversion of the large numbers of pagans still living in the eastern Pyrenees.[15]

The Muslim conquests of 711–18 destroyed the Visigothic kingdom. Northeastern Spain fell under the influence either of the new invaders or of the Frankish kingdom. Much of the northern half of the Peninsula was a staging point for Muslim military operations which eventually spilled over the Pyrenees into the southern ranges of the Merovingian realm, only to be slowly driven back by such Frankish leaders as Charles Martel in the mideighth century. This Christian drive southward was capped by the victories of Charlemagne (769–814) and Louis the Pious (814–40), which brought most of the Catalan coast as far south as Barcelona into the Carolingian orbit. This new territory quickly came to be called the Spanish March or *marca hispanica*.[16]

The uneasy stalemate between Christian and Muslim in the Spanish March, along with the distance of this battle zone from the core of Carolingian administration, made the delegation of power a fact of Iberian political life. Members of eminent Visigothic and Frankish families bearing the title of count or marquis held temporary dominion over the Spanish lands in the name of the Carolingian sovereign. Such marcher agents tended to transfer their official jurisdictions into heritable allodial tenures on which they founded or advanced their noble status. The beginnings of a regional social consciousness and political identity also stirred among the general population. Long referred to by the Franks as *hispani*, the Visigothic refugees had first settled in southern France shortly after the Islamic

---

14. Harold Livermore, *The Origins of Spain and Portugal* (London: Allen and Unwin. 1971), 39, 69; Roger Collins, *Early Medieval Spain: Unity in Diversity, 400–1000* (New York: St. Martin's Press, 1983), 34, 42, 54, 107–8; Leonard A. Curchin, *Roman Spain: Conquest and Assimilation* (London: Routledge, 1991), 57.

15. Jaime Vicens Vives, *Approaches to the History of Spain*, trans. Joan Connelly Ullmann (Berkeley: University of California Press, 1967), 23.

16. Derek W. Lomax, *The Reconquest of Spain* (London: Longman, 1978), 13, 33, 114; Roger Collins, *The Arab Conquest of Spain, 710–797* (London: Blackwell, 1989), 210–16.

conquest. They held land from the Franks in a system known as the *aprisio*. By this arrangement, a cultivator gained full possession of undeveloped land if he worked it for a prescribed period. This same form of land settlement was carried into the *marca hispanica* by the *hispani* who accompanied the Carolingian invaders back into the Peninsula.[17] Thus from the pockets of native noble power along the Pyrenees and among the scattered peasant communities in the isolated uplands, a new society was crystallizing which from 844 even the Carolingian Emperor was forced to recognize.[18]

In spite of this growing social cohesion, the political reality of all the emerging realms of Christian *Iberia* remained distinctly hostile to centralization of any kind. Even the configuration of authority in the Spanish March militated against a single ruler. In political terms, the region was a cluster of comital and viscomital domains which recognized no overlord other than the distant Carolingian Emperor.[19] In a very real sense, then, Catalan political history until well into the thirteenth century was bound up with the struggle for superiority on the part of one section of the land over all others. The chief agent of this conflict was an important Visigothic family of Urgel and Carcassonne, certain of whose members from the ninth century had acted as Carolingian delegated rulers in a number of counties of the Spanish March, including Barcelona, Ausona, and Gerona. From this authority base, the first count of Barcelona, Wifred I the Hairy (873–98), followed two distinct paths to the domination of the *marca hispanica* — the conquest of neighboring Muslim territory and the extension of suzerainty over adjacent Christian counties. Both of these aims were furthered by an extensive castle building program which is reputed to have given Catalonia its name as "the land of castellans."[20]

While Wifred set Barcelona on the road to dominion of its Catalan

17. François Louis Ganshof, "The Last Period of Charlemagne's Reign: A Study in Decomposition," *The Carolingians and the Frankish Monarchy*, trans. Janet Sondheimer (Ithaca, NY: Cornell University Press, 1971), 90–91; Archibald Lewis, *The Development of Southern French and Catalan Society, 718–1050* (Austin: University of Texas Press, 1965), 70–82.

18. *Cartas de población y franquicia de Cataluña*, 2 vols., ed. José María Font Rius (Barcelona-Madrid: Escuela de Estudios Medievales, Publicaciónes de Sección de Barcelona, 1969), 1: doc. 2, pp. 5–7. The capitulary of Charles the Lame in 844 granted a limited legal autonomy to all living "in the Spanish region" (*partibus Hyspania*).

19. Thomas N. Bisson, *The Medieval Crown of Aragon: A Short History* (Oxford: Oxford University Press, 1986), 19–28: José Antonio, *Estudios de la historia del pensamiento español*, 2 vols. (Madrid: Ediciones Cultura Hispanica, 1972; reprint, 1983), 2: 437–50. Catalan rulers used the regnal years of the kings of Francia to mark the dates of their documents until well into the twelfth century.

20. Ramón d'Abadal i de Vinyals, *Els primers comtes catalans*, HC, I, 121–55; Pierre Bonnassie, "Sur la formation du féodalisme Catalan et sa première expansion (jusqu'à 1150 environ)," *EG*, 21; Bonnassie, *From Slavery to Feudalism in South-Western Europe*, trans. Jean Birrell (Cambridge: Cambridge University Press, 1991), 168.

environs and surrounding Muslim territory, his immediate successors were forced from this prudent course by a series of disasters which almost overwhelmed the dynasty. His grandson Borrell II (951–993), seeing no advantage in alliance with a distant and ineffective king of Francia, "separated from the kingdom of the Franks" and took Caliph al-Hakam II of Córdoba (961–976) as lord.[21] When the Muslim ruler died with only a small son to succeed him, one of the young caliph's officials (later given the sobriquet "he who has been made victorious by Allah" (*al-Mansur bi'llah*) established a number of sweeping reforms, including the creation of an effective army. From 977, this new force harried the Christian states of the Peninsula to the very breaking point. In 985 al-Mansur unleashed his professional troops on Catalonia. With no possibility of Carolingian assistance, Borrell II faced the Muslim invasion with a makeshift host which was easily defeated by the Muslim veterans. Barcelona now lay open to the invaders, and on July 6, 985 this "most noble of cities" was sacked and, like most of Christian Spain, left for dead.[22] Yet with al-Mansur's death in 1002, his reforms fell into disrepair, and by 1013 Muslim *Hispania* was fragmented into smaller political units, the *ta'ifas*, which were ruled by the kings of the factions, former governors or agents of the caliph.[23] In a mere thirty years, the Iberian situation had drastically altered, and Christian realms, once under constant threat of attack by the infidel, had taken the offensive and would shortly initiate one of the most important phases of the *reconquista*.

Before Catalonia was ready for such foreign enterprises, however, a broadened local sovereignty base was essential. Such a development seemed impossible in the anarchic environment of early eleventh-century Catalonia. The network of castles that dominated Catalonia unleashed "a measured reign of terror" by the castellans on the surrounding populace and defied all central control — even from the lords who had built the castles.[24]

21. d'Abadal i de Vinyals, *Primers Comtes*, 316–27.

22. *CSJP* chap. 26, p. 45; *GCB* chap. 3, p. 6; Santiago Sobreques, *Els grans comtes de Barcelona*, HC, 2: 7–10; Reinhart Pieter Anne Dozy, *Spanish Islam: A History of the Muslims in Spain*, trans. Francis Griffin Stokes (London: Chatto and Windus, 1913; London: Frank Cass, 1972), 492–96; Manuel Rovira i Sola, "Notes documentales sobre alguns effectes de la presa de Barcelona per al-Mansur," *Acta Histórica et Arqueológico Medievalia*, 1 (1980):31–45.

23. David Wasserstein, *The Rise and Fall of the Party-Kings* (Princeton NJ: Princeton University Press, 1985), 38–39, 42–43; Pierre Bonnassie, *La Catalogne du milieu du Xe à la fin du XIe siècle: Croissance et mutations d'une société*, 2 vols. (Toulouse: Associations des Publications de l'Université de Toulouse de Monail, 1975–76), 2: 612–35, 648–56; Santiago Sobreques i Vidal, *Els barons de Catalunya*, HC 3: 30–31.

24. Pierre Bonnassie, "Du Rhône à la Galicie: Génèse et modalités du régime féodal," *Structures féodales*, 21–23; Bonnassie, *From Slavery to Feudalism*, 107–9; Bonnassie, *La Catalogne*, 596–600.

The Count of Barcelona, Berenguer Ramón I (1017–35), vilified in his own land as "a weak knight . . . of little strength," conducted few campaigns in Muslim Hispania and thus commanded neither golden tribute from the rulers of the *ta'ifas* nor respect from his own great men. Only through the efforts of his mother, Countess Ermessinda, was the Count of Barcelona able to retain his power.[25] The possibility for the extension of comital authority took place during the reign of Berenguer Ramón's son Ramón Berenguer I (1035–76). Spending much of his youth avoiding entanglement in a series of internecine wars among the great lords of Cerdanya, Pallars, and Urgel, this canny ruler capped his advance into adulthood by suppressing a two-decade long revolt by his cousin Mir Geribert in 1059.[26] Attracting an increasing body of support, the Count was able to maneuver all of the Catalan barons into formal recognition of his overlordship. As suzerain of all the great nobles of the Spanish March, the Count strongly asserted his role as the principal judge of the land and surrounded himself with legal advisers who "judged, heard suits, and made rulings according to the [Gothic] laws."[27] He also felt confident enough to take measures of pacification not confined to the feudal sphere. In 1064 and 1068, he adapted the clerical peace and truce to civil ends. The importance of this action cannot be over-stressed since the *pax et treuga* gave the count of Barcelona enhanced ruling possibilities not only as a national protector but also as a national legislator. As Thomas Bisson has rightly pointed out, the peace and truce laid the legal guidelines for Catalonia's "constitutional order" down into the thirteenth century.[28]

Though the reign of Ramón Berenguer I set the stage for the advance of his comital office on all fronts, this foundation of power was not built on until the eve of the twelfth century. In the intervening three bloody decades, several assassinations within the count of Barcelona's family brought his land to the brink of civil strife.[29] With the reign of Ramón Berenguer III

25. *GCB* chap. 9, p. 27; Sobreques i Vidal, *Grans comtes*, 26–31; Prospero Bofarull y Moscaró, *Los condes de Barcelona vindicados y cronología y genealogía de los reyes de España*, 2 vols. (Barcelona: Imprenta de J. Oliveres y Montmany, 1836; Barcelona: La Vanguardia, 1988), 1: 251–54, 275–76.

26. *GCB* chap. 11, p. 32; *CSJP* chap. 29, p. 47; Sobreques Vidal, *Els barons de Catalunya*, 30–31.

27. Bonnassie, *Catalogne* 2: 705–11; Josep Trenchs Odena, "La escríbania de Ramón Berenguer III (1097–1131)," *Saitabi* 31(1984):12.

28. Thomas N. Bisson, "The Organized Peace in Southern France and Catalonia, ca. 1140 – ca. 1230," *AHR* 82(1977): 291.

29. *GCB* chap. 4, p. 7; *CSJP* chaps. 29–30, pp. 47–49; Bofarull y Moscaró, *Los condes*, 2: 114–16. In 1071, Ramón Berenguer I's first son Pere Ramón murdered his stepmother Almodis, described variously as a "distinguished, illustrious queen" and a "woman of sad,

(1097–1131), however, the possibilities of a greater Catalonia began to emerge. Ironically, many of the early territorial gains of this young man — "very pleasant, generous, and accomplished in arms" — came into his hands without the drawing of a sword. In 1111 and 1117 respectively, the count fell heir to the small but strategic Pyrenean counties of Besalú and Cerdanya, leaving only two other major sections of the old *marca hispanica* outside the direct control of the Barcelona house.[30] In 1112 he concluded a marriage with Countess Douce of Provence which would eventually extend the influence of the Barcelona house beyond the Pyrenees.

Profiting from the disarry of Muslim *ta'ifas* that bordered his lands, Ramón Berenguer III followed his predecessors' policy of extorting "yearly tribute" (*parias*) from the rulers of these states, who paid these sums in the misguided hope that the Iberian Christian states would accept their cash in lieu of their land. Such tribute money did not, however, prevent the count from engaging in such urban reclamation schemes as the resettlement of the long-ruined town of Tarragona in 1118. Nor did the flow of Muslim gold northward into the count's coffers dissuade his people from slowly recovering territory in the no man's land between his own realm and the *ta'ifas* of Lerida and Tortosa.[31] Rather than closing ranks against the invaders, the Muslim kinglets were their own worst enemies, often allying with Christian forces against their coreligionists. It was widely and bitterly asserted among contemporary Muslim intellectuals that both Christian greed and the immorality of their own people had "weakened the bonds of the community of the Prophet."[32]

With such an atmosphere of general despair, it is little wonder that *ta'ifa* society fell under the severe influence of the Almoravids. This Berber dynasty had gained control of the majority of North Africa before it inter-

---

unbridled lewdness." In 1082 one of the old count's other sons, Berenguer Ramón II, was implicated in the foul ambush and murder of his sibling Ramón Berenguer II. For their bloody actions, these murderers within the confines of the first family of the land were characterized by the *Gesta Comitum Barchinonensium* as

a pair of vipers, who after they had naturally broken from their mothers' wombs, killed them.

30. *GCB* chap. 4, p. 7; Joseph F. O'Callaghan, *A History of Medieval Spain* (Ithaca, NY: Cornell University Press, 1975), 218; Bernard F. Reilly, *The Medieval Spains* (Cambridge: Cambridge University Press, 1993), 107.

31. *GCB* chap. 4, p. 8; *La documentación pontificia hasta Inocencio III, 965–1216*, ed. Demetrio Mansilla y Reoyo *Monumenta Hispaniae Vaticana*, 1 (Rome: Instituto Español de Estudios Eclesiásticos, 1955), docs. 29–30, pp. 46–48; José Goñi Gaztambide, *História de la bula de cruzada en España, Victoriensia*, 4 (Vittoria: Editorial del Seminario, 1958), 55–59.

32. Wasserstein, *Party Kings*, 279–81.

vened in Hispanic affairs with the impressive victory over a joint Christian army at Zallaqa in 1086.[33] When the count was forced to beat back a Muslim invasion on his own soil in 1108, his stance toward Muslim Spain entered a distinctly warlike phase that culminated in 1114 with a crusade against the Balearic Islands. Conquering a portion of the chain's largest island, Majorca, he could only hold it for a year because the Muslim population so outnumbered his own forces.[34] Despite this setback, a clear precedent of territorial aggrandizement at the expense of the infidel had been established. It would not be lost on the next count of Barcelona, Ramón Berenguer IV.

The new count, like his counterpart in Aragon Alfonso I the Battler (1104–34), was passionately committed to the war on Islam and in 1134 dedicated himself for a full year to the service of the military religious order of the Templars.[35] With these martial goals firmly fixed before him, Ramón Berenguer proceeded to lay plans for the invasion of the two major *ta'ifas* that bordered his land. These aims came to fruition in 1148 and 1149 when he commanded a polyglot crusading army in the conquest of Tortosa and Lerida.[36]

The rapidity of Ramón Berenguer IV's conquests starkly emphasized how different were the lands he now ruled. In Old Catalonia, the descendant of the Spanish March, the feudal and principal order imposed by Ramón Berenguer "the Old" in the 1060s and 1070s was largely locked in place. In the newly-conquered territory, New Catalonia, a brand of feudalism existed but lords exercised fewer quasi-public rights, and vassals on all levels received extensive privileges and exemptions as an inducement to settle the new lands. Both sections were tied together by the count of Barcelona's claim to rule them by virtue of his office of *princeps*. Despite the differences between these two regions, a political unity was beginning to

33. Charles Julian Bishko, "The Spanish and Portuguese Reconquest," *A History of the Crusades*, ed. Kenneth M. Setton et al., 6 vols. (Madison: University of Wisconsin Press, 1962–75), 3: 400–405; Lomax, *Reconquest*, 55–58, 68–78, 83; Wasserstein, *Party Kings*, 288–99; Reilly, *Medieval Spains*, 97.

34. Lomax *Reconquest*, 55–58; Goñi Gaztambide *Historia*, 68–69; Wasserstein *Party Kings*, 285–87.

35. ACA, Pergaminos de Ramón Berenguer IV, no. 28; *CDACA* 4: doc. 11, pp. 29–33; Alan J. Forey, *The Templars in the Corona de Aragon* (London: Oxford University Press, 1973), 17; Forey, *The Military Orders From the Twelfth to the Early Fourteenth Centuries* (Toronto: University of Totonto Press, 1992), 24.

36. Caffaro, *De captione Almerie et Tortuose*, ed. Antonio Ubieto Arteta (Valencia: Anubar, 1973), 30–35; Bishko, "Spanish and Portuguest Reconquest," 409–11; Lomax, *Reconquest*, 93.

form between them, and this unity largely resided in their allegiance to the count of Barcelona as sovereign.[37] A similar kind of monarchical unity in regnal diversity developed in 1137 when the marriage of Ramon Berenguer IV to Queen Petronilla of Aragon lashed two very different countries to the will of one ruler.[38]

Catalonia: The Bonds and Divisions of a Nascent Society

The prototype for all the realms of Christian Iberia was the defunct but partially remembered Visigothic kingdom. A view of this state and its institutions is preserved in the monumental Visigothic law code of the region, the "Book of Judges" (*Liber Judiciorum*; *Fuero Juzgo*) which constituted the prime legal text throughout the Christian portions of the Peninsula until the eleventh century.[39] With the sudden demise of the Visigothic kingdom, other influences gradually came into play. In the land that became Catalonia, Frankish political forms soon grew to dominate. An "official" nobility emerged from the remnants of the Visigothic noble class, and other wealthy hispani who acted as Frankish agents. These "princes" (*principes*) or "wielders of public authority" (*potestates*) generated the ruling families in each of the Catalan counties, including Barcelona.[40] In reality, however, the exigencies of Catalonia as a frontier zone ringed by infidel enemies prevented the immediate duplication of a strong Visigothic-type monarchy and nobility. Instead, small farming communities developed in the countryside and around the largely-deserted urban sites.[41] This

37. José Maria Font Rius, "La comarca de Tortose a raiz de la reconquista cristiana (1148)," *CHE* 19(1953): 165; Bisson, "Feudalism," 175–85.

38. Joaquim Traggia, "Illustración del reynado de don Ramiro de Aragón," *MRAH* 3(1799): docs. 13–14, pp. 598–91; *CDACA* 4: docs. 26–27, pp. 62–64; Josep Pererna i Espelt, "Les condiciones de la unió de Aragó i Catalunya en un manuscrit de Valencia Rafael Martí de Viciana," *Arxiu de Textos Catalans Antics* 2(1983): 357–61.

39. Michel Zimmermann, "L'usage du droit wisigothique en Catalogne du IXe au XIIe siècle," *Mélanges de la Casa de Velasquez* 9(1973): 233–70; Anscari M. Mundó, "Els manuscrits del 'Liber judiciorum' de las comarques gironines," *EG*, 77–86; Walter Kienast, "La pervivencia del derecho godo en el sur de Francia y Cataluña," *BRABLB* 35(1973–4): 265–74; Teofilo F. Ruiz, "Law, Spanish," *DMA* 7: 519–20.

40. Bonnassie, *La Catalogne*, 1: 154–60, 165–66; d'Abadal, *Primers comtes*, 250–55; Sobreques Vidal, *Els Barons*, 1–2; Archibald Lewis, "Count Gerald of Aurillac and Feudalism in South Central France in the Early Tenth Century," *Traditio* 20(1969): 48, n. 43.

41. Pierre Bonnassie, "A Family of the Barcelona Countryside and its Economic Activities Around the Year 1000," *Early Medieval Society*, ed. Slyvia Thrupp (New York: Appleton-Century-Croft, 1967), 108–11; Bonnassie, "Formation," 10.

"society of free men" generally owned their own land and had some degree of power in the communal groups they were part of.[42] By the mid-eleventh century, the Catalan countryside had changed from a scene of allodial land tenure and peasant liberty to one dominated by castles and those who staffed them. The castellans and garrisons were effectively supported by the land and population that surrounded the fortress. While the castellans were obliged to turn over control of their fortresses to the "official" lords who owned them, they increasingly retained these strongholds as their own bases. A corps of professional warriors, uncontrolled even by their own overlords, was thus unleashed on the surrounding rural population.[43]

Between the sack of Barcelona in 985 and the victory of Ramón Berenguer "the Old" over his last principal rival in 1059, the "militarization" of Catalan society, to use Archibald Lewis's phrase, took place. Relations between weak and strong men were established in the Spanish March by the adoption of Carolingian forms of allegiance and conditional service in exchange for lordly grants of land.[44] In the world of shifting alliances and rivalries that comprised eleventh-century Catalonia, the pressing need for loyalty was accomplished by the linkage of vassalic dependence to feudal tenancy. The personal alliance was solemnly realized in the ceremony of "homage" (*hominaticum*) in which one man acknowledged himself to be a lord's man, or vassal. To seal the pact, the vassal took an oath of "fealty" (*fidelitas, affidamentum*) which was properly sanctified by having the oath-taker touch the Gospels or stand on an altar during the ceremony.[45] By this ritual, the vassal, whether noble or not, formally promised to safeguard the life and limb of his lord, hold fiefs and castles granted by his master according to conditions acceptable to both parties, and finally to be the lord's "helper, with righteous faith and without deceit." The lord, for his part, swore to defend his vassal, maintain his rights and provide for his well-being.[46] The most tangible and significant result of homage and fealty was

42. Bonnassie, "Formation," 9–10; Bonnassie, *From Slavery to Feudalism*, 152–53.

43. Archibald Lewis, "Cataluña como frontera militar (870–1050)," *AEM* 5 (1968): 26–27; Lewis, *Development*, 238–39.

44. *The Cambridge History of Medieval Political Thought*, ed. James Henderson Burns (Cambridge: Cambridge University Press, 1988), 200; *The History of Feudalism*, ed. David Herlihy (New York: Walker, 1970; London: Macmillan, 1971), 84–85, 103–4; François Louis Ganshof, *Feudalism*, trans. Philip Grierson (London: Longman, 1952; New York: Harper and Row, 1961), 3–11.

45. Bonnassie, *La Catalogne*, 2: 741–43.

46. Bonnassie, "Formation," 14; Trenchs Odena, "La escribanía," 36; Marc Bloch, "European Feudalism," *Theories of Society: Foundations of Modern Sociological Theory*, ed. Talcott Parsons et al., 2 vols. (New York: Free Press, 1961, reprint, 1966), 387–88; *History of Feudalism*, doc. 14, p. 97; *A Source Book of Mediaeval History*, ed. Frederick Austin Ogg (New

the lord's investiture of his vassal with a fief. Up until the eleventh century, the *fevum* or *terra de feo* was a grant of fiscal land made to various types of vassals, including officials and castellans. Despite differences in terminology, the fief in Catalonia was considered by the 1050s the opposite of the alod. The *fevum* personalized the relationship between lord and vassal. The commendation of a fief gave the vassal only provisional "control" (*potestas*) over it. He promised orally and in the written "pact" (*convenientia*) that he would relinquish such custody whenever requested by the lord and would not usurp or legally contest ownership of the fief "whether at war ar at peace with his lord" (*iratus et pacatus*).[47] The fief, as the core of a relationship of mutual allegiance and duty, was fated to outlast the alliance that brought it into being. While the investiture of feudal land was initially only for the lifetime of the vassal, the bond formalized by the granting of such land did not normally expire with a vassal's death, since his place could be taken by his son or nearest male relative. From this ongoing connection between lordly and vassalic families, the steps to the heritability and finally alienability of fiefs were short ones.[48] The viability of the "system" was lessened as the feudal holding became more important than the feudal relationship. The drive to gain as many fiefs as possible often left a vassal with more than one lord. Even with the emergence of "liege vassalage" (*solidancia*) in eleventh-century Catalonia, the temptation to garner a number of fiefs gave the same vassal more than one "liege lord" (*melior senior*) whom he was bound to honor above all others. The situation might be further complicated if his best lords were implacable enemies and thus he had to choose one over the other for battle service.[49] This constant fragmentation of fidelity perpetuated the kind of anarchy that had given rise to feudal forms in the first place. The regime of Catalan castles as well as the feudal

York: Cooper Square Publishers, 1907, reprint, 1972), doc. 37, pp. 220–21. The relationship of lord and vassal was delineated very early on by such writers as Fulbert of Chartres. In 1024, the Bishop wrote to Duke William IV of Aquitaine concerning lordly and vassalic duties. The vassal was to defend, counsel, and aid his lord in every way possible. Lords were also bound to treat their vassals in the same way. If either party failed to carry out these obligations, they were guilty of perjury against the oath and pact which tied them together.

47. Bonnassie, *La Catalogne*, 2: 739–40, 748–49; Bonnassie, "Formation," 13; Richard W. Southern, *The Making of the Middle Ages* (New Haven, CT: Yale University Press, 1953; reprint, 1968), 111; Joseph Strayer, "Feudalism," *DMA* 5: 52; Eulalia Rodón Binué, *El lenguaje técnico del feudalismo en el siglo XI en Cataluña; Contribucion al estudio de latin medieval*, Escuela de filología de Barcelona: filología clásica 16 (Barcelona: Concejo Superior de Investigaciónes Científicas, 1957), 184.

48. Bloch, "European Feudalism," 387–90.

49. Bonnassie, *La Catalogne*, 2: 743–48; Bonnassie, "Formation," 15; Bonnassie, *From Slavery to Feudalism*, 159; Strayer, "Feudalism," 5: 55.

relationships that tied castellans up to the old nobility and down to the peasantry was in sore need of ordering. This drive for a reestablishment of public authority came from two different directions. With the accession of Ramón Berenguer I in 1035, the count of Barcelona began consistently reasserting his role of public authority. His actual power, however, was often not great enough to suppress the rampant violence which held the Catalan countryside in its grip and so another institution of the old order, the Church, had to step in and try to regulate the society it served.

As the tyranny of castles over the Catalan rural districts deepened, two populations emerged — one skilled in the use of arms and the other largely unarmed. The "helpless" (*inermis*) group largely consisted of churchmen and peasants. Though both groups fell under the castle's domination, the former had an authority and property base from which to operate while the latter did not. The personal status of the peasants did not always change, but the control over their own lives most assuredly did. They might remain free, but they were also weighed down with burdens onerous enough to pose a constant threat to their liberty. In addition to the growing number of services peasants owed to their immediate lord which, in time came to be know as the "evil customs" (*mals usos*), they suffered largely in silence from the depredations of the castle warriors.[50]

The second division of the largely unarmed population, the clergy, began to exercise a new influence in this changing society. Often large landowners who depended on peasant labor, the churchmen were not inclined to allow the destruction of public peace, especially when clerical institutions were engulfed in the unending waves of castellan violence. Though most of the great churchmen sprang from the region's old nobility, they did not turn to the path of arms to defend the "helpless" population but fell back instead on Carolingian traditions of civil protection of church lands.[51] When public authority could not contain a social violence which held nothing to be sacred, the Catalan clergy took matters in their own hands. Turning to the "Peace of God" (*pax Dei*), a form that had developed in the southern French clerical circles in the tenth century, the Catalan

50. Paul Freedman, *The Origins of Peasant Servitude in Medieval Catalonia* (Cambridge: Cambridge University Press, 1991), 17–18.

51. *El archivo condal de Barcelona en los siglos IX–X* (Barcelona: Concejo Superior de Investicaciónes Científicas, 1951), doc. 11, pp. 121–23; Roger Collins, "Charles the Bald and Wilfrid the Hairy," *Charles the Bald: Court and Kingdom*, ed. Margaret T. Gibson and Janet L. Nelson (Oxford: Oxford University Press, 1981; Roger Collins, *Law, Culture, and Regionalism in Early Medieval Spain* (Aldershot: Variorum Reprints, 1990), 179; *CSCV* 3: docs. 913, 920, pp. 101–2, 107.

churchmen adapted it to their homeland. At a number of small assemblies between 1027 and 1068, the prelates of the Catalan counties, led by Bishop Oliba of Ausona, established peace laws within their own dioceses. The statutes which emerged from these meetings declared the zones around churches, monastic sites, and cemeteries to be "circles of peace." They also proclaimed protection for all of the unarmed people in their ecclesiatical zone of jurisdiction and their property. In a uniquely Catalan development, the clergy established a *treuga* or truce for the holiest periods of the ecclesiastical year. Though excommunication was threatened for those who violated the peace or truce, malefactors were perhaps slowed but not deterred by the fear that their actions might ultimately cost them salvation. Without armed force to bring violent criminals to justice, the *pax et treuga* constituted more of a moral deterrent than a complete judicial response to the endemic violence of eleventh-century Catalonia.[52]

While the spread of feudal ties and the proclamation of the peace and truce were makeshift answers from the ranks of a Catalan society that was itself falling apart, the final response to the disintegration came from the count of Barcelona, whose weakness had initially allowed the localization of authority which centered on individual castles. By a slow process of asserting his power and authority on the basis of his long neglected roles as high judge and protector of his people, the count began to expand his power by virtue of his superior legal claim. A milestone in this journey was the creation of the *Usatges of Barcelona*.

Custom into Law in the High Middle Ages

From the late Empire of the fifth century to the rebirth of Roman legal studies in the twelfth century, written territorial laws and non-written local custom existed side by side in all the emerging societies of Europe.[54] With the withering of public authority in the tenth century, the place of royal statutory law was largely taken by feudal custom as well as by the ecclesiasti-

52. Walter Ullmann, "The Medieval Papal Court as an International Tribunal," *Virginia Journal of International Law* 11 (1971): 363; Elisabeth Vodola, *Excommunication in the Middle Ages* (Berkeley: University of California Press, 1986), 38–39, 44–69; Bisson, "Organized Peace," 305.

54. Guterman, *From Personal ro Territorial Institutiones*, 17–38; Zacour, *Introduction to Medieval Institutions*, 123; Patrick Wormald, "*Lex Scripta* and *Verbum Regis*, from Euric to Cnut," *Early Medieval Kingship*, ed. Patrick H. Sawyer and Ian N. Wood (Leeds: The Editors, 1977), 111.

cal peace and truce. As rulers began to reassert their claims to supremacy in the eleventh and twelfth centuries, they came to view the control of law in all of its aspects as a viable means of attaining a broadened base of allegiance. Legislation, which proclaimed the sovereign's "care over the commonwealth," also reasserted a lapsed public role that effectively cut across feudal and class lines.[55] Though many great nobles contested this royal claim to a legal and judicial monopoly, the assertion of the rulers that they were the definers and administrators of law gave regnal power a base that solidified as these judicial and legislative functions increasingly were claimed to be the exclusive business of the Crown and its officials.[56] Since most of Europe lived under unwritten legal usage, these customary norms passed into the realm of written law through the legislative efforts of the sovereign. In reality, the transformation of local usage into a set of statutes binding on an entire territory constituted the most significant form of legislation by European rulers before the thirteenth century.[57] The format and philosophy for such legislation, however, was provided by Rome's law. Though Roman legal studies never really died in isolated intellectual centers of southern France and Italy, the discovery of a near-complete copy of Justinian's *Digest* in the eleventh century reawoke the investigation of Imperial jurisprudence across the Continent.[58] Roman law, in fact, had a unifying effect on the perception and practice of law as students from across Europe came to Bologna and other centers to learn the "new law." The graduates of such schools attained brilliant careers as judges, notaries, advo-

55. *History of Feudalism*, doc. 38, p. 237; *Cambridge History*, 191–95: Kenneth Pennington, "Law Codes, 1000–1500," *DMA* 7: 425–26.

56. Zacour, *Medieval Institutions*, 129–32; Pennington, "Law Codes," *DMA* 7: 426; André Gouron, "La science juridique française aux XIe et XIIe siècles: Diffusion du droit de Justinien et influences canoniques jusqu'à Gratien," in *Études sur la diffusion des doctrines juridiques médiévales* (London: Variorum Reprints, 1987), 22–23.

57. Theodore Frank Thomas Plucknett, "The Relations Between the Roman Law and the English Common Law Down to the Sixteenth Century: A General Survey," *University of Toronto Law Journal* 3(1939–40): 32; Alan Watson, *The Evolution of Law* (Baltimore: Johns Hopkins University Press, 1985), 43–58; Walter Ullmann, *Law and Politics in the Middle Ages: An Introduction to the Sources of Medieval Political Ideas* (Ithaca, NY: Cornell University Press, 1975), 193; William E. Brynteson, "Roman Law and Legislation in the Middle Ages," *Speculum* 41(1966): 430–31; Armin Wolf, "Die Gesetzgebung der Enstehenden Territorialstaaten," *Handbuch*, 1: 553–55.

58. Paul Vinagradoff, *Roman Law in Medieval Europe* (Oxford: Oxford University Press, 1929), 444–47, 56–57; Hans Julius Wolff, *Roman Law: An Historical Introduction* (Norman: University of Oklahoma Press, 1951; reprint, 1976), 188; Charles Donahue, Jr., "Law, Civil — Corpus Juris, Revival and Spread," *DMA* 7: 418–21; Knut Wolfgang Nörr, "Vierter Abschnitt die Kanonistische Literatur," *Handbuch*, 1: 371–72; Nörr, "Institutional Foundations," 324–26; Kuttner, "Revival of Jurisprudence," 300–304.

cates, and officials.[59] The Roman legal training they brought to bear on these posts was of crucial importance in configuring and articulating the emerging administrative institutions they managed. The law of their homelands was also reshaped through their efforts. Thus from the raw material of custom came royal statutes with some of the scope and organization of the old Roman imperial codes. Nowhere are the changes wrought by the renewal of Roman legal studies more evident than among the corps of "civil servants" of the Count of Barcelona who produced the *Usatges of Barcelona*.

The Barcelona Court and the Evolution of the *Usatges*

In spite of the count of Barcelona's victories of the mid-eleventh century, he lived much as his great nobility did. Changing residences every few days, the count was surrounded and served by an equally changeable household. Besides the barons who served as comital companions and advisers, the *curia comitis* was made up of a number of personal servants who increasingly exercised public functions.[60] Clergymen, especially cathedral canons, wrote official documents and served as judges for the count's tribunals.[61] While these men were almost entirely drawn from the region's clergy, many of them took only minor orders. In reality, they became as closely identified with their judicial or educational activities as with their clerical offices. Thus more than one "grammarian" (*grammaticus*), "professor" (*doctor*), or "schoolmaster" (*caput schole*) served the count in rendering judgments and

59. Vinagradoff, *Roman Law*, 77–78; Plucknett, *Relations*, 35; Ernst Levy, "The Reception of Highly-Developed Legal Systems by People of Different Cultures," *Washington Law Review and State Bar Journal* 25 (1950): 245; Haskins, *Renaissance*, 96–100.

60. Luis García de Valdeavellano y Arcimus, *Curso de história de los institución es españoles de los origenes al final de la edad media* (Madrid: Revista de Occidente, 1968), 495; Jaime Caruana Gómez de Barreda, "Los mayordomos de Aragón en los siglos XII y XIII," *RABM* 62 (1956): 350–51; Jesús María Lalinde Abadía, *La jurisdicción real inferior en Cataluña* (*"Corts," "Veguers," "Batlles"*) (Barcelona: Ayuntamiento de Barcelona, 1970), 89.

61. José Balari Jovany, *Orígenes históricos de Cataluña*, 2 vols. (Barcelona: Hijos de J. Jepus, 1899; Abadia de San Cugat de Valls: Instituto Internaciónal de Cultura Romanica, 1964), 2: 471–79; José Bono, *Historia del derecho notarial español*, 2 vols. (Madrid: Junta de Decanos de los Colegios Notariales de España, 1979), 1: 118–21; Ferran de Sagarra i de Siscar, *Sigiliografia catalan: Inventari, descriptió, i estudi del segells de Catalunya*, 5 vols. (Barcelona: Estampa d'Henrich, 1915–32), 1: 39; Ferran Valls Taberner, "El liber iudicum popularis de Homobonus de Barcelona," *Obras*, 2: 245–46; *Usatges de Barcelona*, ed. Ramon d'Abadal i de Vinyals and Ferran Valls Taberner, *Texts de Dret Català* 1 (Barcelona: Diputació Provincial, 1913), xiv–xv; Bonnassie, *La Catalogne*, 2: 709–11; Trenchs Odena, "La escribanía", 14–15.

in drawing up important documents.[62] In effect, a civil *cursus honorum* began to open up for such clerics at the same time as their ecclesiastical careers advanced.[63] The count of Barcelona's court entered into a new phase of complexity and professionalism after the union of Catalonia and Aragon in 1137.[64] The officials of this new composite state were moving toward a professionalism that tied them to the sovereign as well as to the emerging institution that was his court. They were privy to a kind of group memory from court service and effectively constituted a living history of the dynasty they served. The traditions of the count of Barcelona's household were thus squarely in the hands of the officials who administered it.[65] The *Usatges of Barcelona* is a clear case in point. Though the code is a reflection of the legal customs of the Catalan counties subject to the count of Barcelona, it is not an exact copy of these usages. Instead, the region's oral traditions were refashioned and rectified according to the dictates of its literate class. The clergymen in the service of the count employed the "technology of literacy" to glorify their master's political aspirations and to display their own legal erudition.[66] These overriding aims are apparent throughout the *Usatges*.

If, as Alan Watson asserts, "the borrowing of another's law is a very potent means of legal growth," then the investigation of what elements were borrowed and how they were incorporated must reveal in some measure the minds behind the legislation.[67] The legal works cited in the *Usatges of Barcelona* are especially instructive in this regard. To the custom-

---

62. Trenchs Odena, "La escribanía," 17; ACA, Pergaminos de Ramón Berenguer III, nos. 50, 69, 132, 133, 173.

63. Trenchs Odena, "La escribanía," 14, 20; Ferran Valls Taberner, "La cour comtal barcelonaise, " *Obras*, 2: 270–71; ACA, Pergaminos de Ramón Berenguer III, nos. 177, 208, 244; Gouron, "Science française," 28.

64. Josep Trenchs Odena, "Los escribanos de Ramón Berenguer IV. Nuevos datos," *Saitabi* 29(1979): 6; Antonio M. Aragó and José Trenchs Odena, "Las escribanías reales catalano-aragónesas de Ramón Berenguer IV a la minoría de Jaime I," *RABM* 80(1977): 421–22; Luis Felipe Arregui Lucea, "La curia y los cortes en Aragón," *Argensola* 4(1953): 3–4; Thomas N. Bisson, "Ramón de Caldes (c. 1135–c. 1200): Dean of Barcelona and King's Minister," in *Law, Church, and Society: Essays in Honor of Stephen Kuttner*, ed. Kenneth Pennington and Robert Somerville (Philadelphia: University of Pennsylvania Press, 1977), 281–82.

65. Frederick L. Cheyette, "The 'Sale' of Carcassone to the Counts of Barcelona (1067–1070) and the Rise of the Trancavels," *Speculum* 63(1988): 863.

66. Rosamond McKitterick, *The Carolingians and the Written Word* (Cambridge: Cambridge University Press, 1989), 250–51; Janet L. Nelson, "Literacy in Carolingian Government," *The Uses of Literacy in Early Medieval Europe*, ed. Rosamond McKitterick (Cambridge: Cambridge University Press, 1990), 262–63, 270–71; Ian Wood, "Administration, Law, and Culture in Merovingian Gaul," *Uses of Literacy*, 67; Franz H. Baüml, "Varieties and Consequences of Medieval Literacy and Illiteracy," *Speculum* 55(1980): 243–44; Clanchy, *From Memory to Written Record*, 178.

67. Watson, *Evolution of Law*, 93; Pennington, "Law Codes," *DMA* 7: 426.

ary feudal norms that comprise the core of the code, the curials of Ramón Berenguer IV added a sizeable collection of excerpts from other law codes. Since one of the avowed purposes of the code was to complement Visigothic law, it is not surprising that a large number of *Usatges* articles are citations or adaptations of the *Liber Judiciorum (Fuero Juzgo)*.[68] The work of Justinian, whether from the *Corpus Juris Civilis* itself or such later compilations or collections as the *Breviarium Alarici*, the *Petri Exceptiones*, or the *Epitome Aegidii*, was also cited on a number of occasions.[69] Fragments from almost contemporaneous works of legal scholarship also appear in the code, since its authors had recourse to the collections of canon law made by Ivo of Chartres and Gratian and the treatise on feudal law composed by Umberto de Orto.[70] Because of its position as a compendium of all branches of knowledge in the Middle Ages, it is scarcely surprising that certain passages on the nature of law and custom in the *Etymologiae* by Isidore of Seville were also chosen for inclusion in the code.[71]

Though this set of excerpts from laws old and new might superficially seem little more than scholarly window dressing, none of the borrowings were made without reason and, in one way or another, they all demonstrate something of the authors' intentions. Extraneous material was ultimately gathered into the code: (1) to state general legal principles, (2) to clarify doubtful points in Catalan customary law, (3) to address problems which custom made no attempt to solve, and (4) to advance the power of the count of Barcelona by inserting passages from Justinian's *Digest* that asserted that the will of the Emperor was law. The men who brought the *Usatges* into being therefore sought far afield for materials and chose them with some discrimination. In the broader view, these appropriations from other legal systems, some of them of fairly recent vintage, show the erudition and resources of the lawyers who made the code.

The mere fact of so many extrinsic elements within the *Usatges* proves how quickly Catalonia had come under the influence of the study of Roman law and the idea of the learned law. The new legal knowledge was brought into Catalonia by Catalans who had studied abroad and found careers as teachers, officials, and churchmen. Their influence is also reflected by the large influx of legal books into Catalan monastic and cathedral libraries in

---

68. *Usatges*, arts. 2, 34, 89, 96, 118–19, 125, B6, C3, C4, pp. 50, 78, 124–26, 132, 150–54, 170–72.

69. *Usatges*, arts. 65, 72, 80, 85, 118–19, B3, B4, pp. 102, 110, 118, 122, 150–54, 170.

70. *Usatges*, arts. 29, 68, pp. 74, 106.

71. *Usatges*, arts. DI and D2, p. 173.

the first half of the twelfth century. The Visigothic sources were the closest to hand, since multiple copies of the *Liber Judiciorum* and the *Etymologiae* had long existed in the libraries of the region. Though a good number of Roman sources were available because of the political and intellectual ties that bound Catalonia to Provence and Italy,[72] excerpts of the same works were also accessible from the huge collections of canon law which circulated in eastern Spain throughout the later eleventh and twelfth centuries. The most important of these was the *Caesaraugustana*, a wide-ranging compendium of Visigothic, canon, and Roman law compiled in the early twelfth century. According to Carlo Guido Mor, this work was brought into being by "a canonist of eclectic tendency" and very well may have exerted the same kind of influence over the fashioning of the *Usatges* as it surely did for that of the *Exceptiones Petri*.[73]

After sifting through the work of the men who brought the *Usatges* project to completion, what can be said of them and the nature of their work? Since the code was not a uniform one that came into being at any one time, but was rather, as Thomas Bisson says, "a compilation of compilations," a number of minds brought it to completion.[74] It is likely that the court rules (referred to variously as *usatici* and *usualia*) that surfaced during the reign of Ramón Berenguer "the Old" were written only in the most rudimentary or abbreviated form and then solely for courtroom use. The keepers of this body of customary legal precedent were thus presumably the judges who used it to render proper verdicts. The full breadth of their knowledge in the pronouncements of customary law came not from peering over legal tomes but rather from long years of experience in their masters' tribunals. As the twelfth century passed, the "lawmen" visible in the Barcelona court increasingly became "bookmen" as well. Most of them were familiar with the new trends of legal scholarship, and at least one of

72. Balari, 2: 506; Eduardo de Hinojosa y Naveros, "La admisión del derecho romano en Cataluña," *Obras*, 3 vols. (Madrid, Concejo Superior de Investigaciónes Científicas, 1948), 393–94.

73. Ferran Valls Taberner, "Les col.leccions canoniques a Catalunya durant l'època comtal (1072–1162)," *Obras*, 2: 104–6; Alfonso Garcia Gallo, *Manual de Historia del Derecho Español*, 2 vols. (Madrid: Artes Graficas Ediciones, 1975; reprint, 1984), 1: 387–88; Carlo Guido Mor, "En torno de la formación del texto de los 'usatici barchinonae'," *AHDE* 7–8(1957–58): 444; Guillermo Maria de Broca y Montagut, "Juristes y Jurisconsults Catalans del Segles XI, XII, y XIII: Fonts del seus coneixements y transcendencia," *Anuari* 2(1908): 431; Kenneth Pennington, "Petri Exceptiones," *DMA* 9: 544; Roger E. Reynolds, "Law, Canon: To Gratian," *DMA* 7: 412; Gouron, "Science française," 57–64; André Gouron, "Aux origines de l'influence des glossateurs en Espagne," Gouron, *Études*, 343–44.

74. Thomas N. Bisson, "The Problem of Feudal Monarchy: Aragon, Catalonia, and France," *Speculum* 53(1978): 467.

them might have received part of his legal training at Bologna. This can be said with some certainty because of the inclusion of passages from the *Libri Feudorum* in the more finished versions of the *Usatges*. The "Book of Fiefs" had only come into use as a textbook at Bologna after 1130. Its insertion in the *Usatges* some two decades later thus points to one of two possibilities: (1) one of the code's authors had studied and taken notes on the "Book of Fiefs" while attending lectures at Bologna, or (2) he used such summaries of the work made and brought back by another student.[75]

All in all, Balari's discussion of the curials who brought the *Usatges* to completion can serve as a starting point for their description:

> whoever redacted the code was not a warrior who clutched a sword and wore armor of steel. Its author, who had a very lofty idea of what it was to be a prince and then elevated the status of prince to a category of almost being a divine state, necessarily had to be an ecclesiastic very well versed in . . . the Sacred Scriptures.[76]

The mere fact of so many churchmen trained in Roman and canon law sought careers in the count of Barcelona's service during the twelfth century enhances the possibility that one or more of them turned his skills to the task of finishing the code. That they were extremely knowledgeable in biblical exegesis also seems certain when their scholarly lives are reviewed. Some, like Renallus, combined the activities of legist, theologian, and historian while serving as the chancellor of Ramón Berenguer III's court.[77] The official documents such members of the court drafted and sometimes wrote out in a fine hand clearly indicate their opinion and understanding of the powers and obligations of the Crown. The ruler, in their view, was very much like an Old Testament patriarch or king. He was to rule with faith and justice, and if he failed to so act for all his people, he ran the risk of losing his throne — both from the backlash of his disgruntled subjects and through the efforts of an expansive papacy. In effect, the legitimacy of civil rulers depended on the moral tenor of their official and personal lives. As one comital instrument of 1151 expressed it

75. Hinojosa, "Admisión," 2:391–92; Joaquim Miret y Sans, "Escolars catalans al estudi de Bolonia en la XIII al XIV centuria," *BRABLB* 8(1915): 137–55; Hastings Rashdall, *The Universities of Europe in the Middle Ages*, ed. Frederick Maurice Powicke and Alfred Brothers Emden, 3 vols. (Oxford: Clarendon Press, 1895; New York: Oxford University Press, 1987), 1: 156; André Gouron, "Aux origines," Gouron, *Études*, 327–32, 336–41.

76. Balari, *Orígenes históricos de Cataluña* 2: 486.

77. Trenchs Odena, "Escribanía de Ramón Berenguer III," 20.

it is specially granted to the dignity of the Prince particularly to look after the temporal goods which Divine Clemency temporarily conceded to him so he may honorably grant these to the Church of God.[78]

From the above, it can safely be concluded that the creators of the *Usatges* were both "Romanizing lawyers" (as d'Abadal i de Vinyals claims)[79] and churchmen who bore an idealized view of the monarch (as Balari asserts). They were, in fact, one and the same. As members of the cathedral and monastic communities, their opinions of the king's relationship to his subjects and the law in general were reflections of the ecclesiastical mirror in which they themselves lived. As students of Roman jurisprudence, their perceptions of the Church and the monarchy in the world, far from being drastically altered, were instead clarified. The authors of the *Usatges*, who had harmonized their offices as clergymen, public servants, and legists, were likewise able to reconcile their own roles as churchmen and royal bureaucrats.

If a portrait of the authors of the *Usatges* can be gleaned from their own handiwork, can the same be done for a fuller understanding of the means employed to bring the code to a finished form? If Stanley Fish is to be believed, every statute contains the "interpretive assumptions" that brought it into being.[80] To see how such assumptions created the *Usatges*, we must look to the workings of the Barcelona court. The mechanism of Alfonso II's court of the early 1170s shows that his curials could summon up an "institutional memory" to recall some types of information about the dynasty and the court they served. When this "remembering" was called on to retrieve information from a time predating even the oldest surviving curial, the data could become tainted with unsubstantiated or garbled traditions. Bearing this in mind, how could "the wise, learned men and judges" of Ramón Berenguer IV have formed a code as rich in indigenous and advenient material as the *Usatges*?

For at least a provisional answer, the dual avocation of the code's compilers must be considered. As judges, the erudite officials of Ramón Berenguer I's court became true legists as they made judicial rulings based on the customary law of the count of Barcelona's lands. By their decisions, the "court rules" became true legal precedents. There is little direct evidence

78. ACA, Pergaminos de Ramón Berenguer IV, no. 241.
79. Ramon d'Abadal I de Vinyals, "La vida politica y sus dirigentes," *Historia de España*, ed. Ramón Menendez y Pidal, 37 vols. (Madrid: Espasa-Calpe, 1963–84), 14: xlviii–xlix; Bonnassie, *La Catalogne*, 2: 713, n. 83.
80. Quoted in Baüml, "Medieval Literacy and Illiteracy," 251–52.

of these *usatici* passing into an easily accessible written format during the eleventh century; if they were written at all, it seems that they seldom circulated beyond the circle of judges who kept them as an abbreviated casebook of Barcelona customary law.[81] A fuller redaction of such customary legal norms in the period before the reign of Ramón Berenguer III is militated against by the fact that the Barcelona court did not normally maintain an archive of documents issued under its aegis before the reign of Alfonso II (1162–96). On the other hand, litigants, especially clerical ones, took great pains in maintaining the official papers which they received from comital tribunals.[82] How, then, could the "court rules of customary law" of the eleventh century become the written code which emerged as the *Usatges* of the mid-twelfth century? The largely completed code of the early 1150s could not have developed except in a literate and stable environment. Ramón Berenguer IV's court, constantly on the move and occupied in one extensive campaign after another with Muslim *Hispania*, was hardly the place for the codification of laws on any scale. Instead, almost certainly, the count, flushed with the complete victories over his Muslim neighbors, capped his glorious military career by bringing the *Usatges* project to fulfillment. Though it seems certain that the eleventh-century customary norms were undergoing some type of editing during the early decades of the twelfth century, there are few demarcation points to determine the stages of this process.[83] It is also clear that such an intricate development could not have come to completion in the count's court even though it was carried out by curials. Ramón Berenguer IV seems to have entrusted the completion of the code to his brightest, best educated judges who also happened to be clerics. The great libraries of the cathedrals of Barcelona and Gerona and those of the monasteries of San Cugat de Valles and Ripoll would have been open to the legists, and, in fact, these collections contained most of the legal works woven into the *Usatges*, along with large fonts of judicial records which had been issued to and preserved by each of these institutions. From such relatively stable centers, the *Usatges* were assuredly worked up into their first written form of a more or less official nature. This pattern of legal codification would be repeated on a number of

---

81. For an opposite view of the emergence of the eleventh-century *usualia*, that is, that the *usualia* emerged as a core of full fledged laws during the reign of Ramón Berenguer "the Old," see Frederic Udina Martorell and Antoni Maria Udina i Abelló, "Consideracions a l'entorn del nucli originari dels 'Usatici Barchinonae'," *EG* 92–98.

82. Trenchs Odena, "Escribanía de Ramón Berenguer III," 14–15.

83. Bisson, "Problem", 465–66; Joan Bastardas i Parera, *Sobre la problematica de Usatges de Barcelona* (Barcelona: Real Academia de Buenas Letras de Barcelona, 1977), 35.

occasions during the long reign of Jaime I (1213–76). This great legislator relied on the clerical legists of his court to draw up law codes and they consistently did so in the literate environment of their religious houses.[84]

The Path of *Usatges* Solidification: From Court Usage to Code

The mapping of the journey of custom into the realm of written law is one fraught with difficulties of terminology and interpretation of that terminology. As legal usage slowly hardens into law, it often comes into writing not as a verifiable, straightforward act of legislation but rather as a reference to customary precedent inserted in the verdict arrived at by judges of a tribunal or within the body of many different types of grants issued by rulers, nobles, and clergy. The variety of names given to the same body of customary law by judge, advocate, or notary only adds to the confusion of carefully monitoring the path custom follows in becoming law.[85]

With these considerations in mind, we may attempt to chart the slow emergence of a Barcelona customary law into a written legal form.[86] Unfortunately, the only ways for gauging this development do not come from the convenient vantage point of hindsight from which the intricate course of custom is seen in its totality. Instead, the only signposts that exist on the road of custom are the incomplete and sometimes conflicting clues left by its definers, the judges. By their decisions, the course of precedent was slowly laid out point by point until a direction of legal procedure and theory eventually turned away from the well-worn path of written, Visigothic law. Even the title which eventually came to be associated with the first codification of the Catalan customary law, *usatici*, had a number of meanings, though each relates to a practice of long duration. Thus a *usaticus* might be: (1) a customary due owed by a vassal to a lord, (2) a tax imposed by a civil or religious authority on the sale of merchandise, or (3) a legal custom.[87] To confuse matters further, synonyms such as *consuetudo* and *mos* (each implying a legal practice of a long-established duration) were used in

84. Jesús María Lalinde Abadía, *Los fueros de Aragón* (Zaragoza: Libreria General, 1979), 54–62.

85. See article D1 of the *Usatges* for Isidore's view of *consuetudo* and *lex*. For discussion of this process in early medieval Europe, see Watson, *Evolution of Law*, 43–61; McKitterick, *The Carolingians and the Written Word*, 37–38.

86. For view of the same process in other European societies, see Wolf, "Gesetzgebung und Kodifikationen," 145–48.

87. Balari, *Orígenes históricos de Cataluña*, 2: 490.

place of *usaticus* in all of its various meanings. With this potential for error in mind, the documentary signals of the evolution of the *Usatges* can be examined.

The great bank of references to the growth of the code were judicial records and the *convenientia* that tied lords and vassals. During the period between Ramón Berenguer I's death in 1076 and the reign of his great-grandson Ramón Berenguer IV, the distinction between Visigothic law and the customs of the Barcelona court was constantly affirmed. Thus in 1070, foral laws were granted to the Pyrenean village of Gerri that conformed on several points with the "custom of the homeland" (*mos patriae*).[88] In 1091, the boundary dispute of two Catalan monasteries was aired before a tribunal of clergymen and nobles headed by Berenguer Ramón II. It was settled "according to the authority of the Gothic law and "the usages of the land" (*usaticos terrae*).[89] During the same period, the difference between the individual acts of municipal lawmaking and the more general customs of the Barcelona court also began to emerge. When, after 1116, Ramón Berenguer III finally honored a papal directive to reclaim Tarragona, one of his first concerns was the establishment of a legal basis for the new settlement. As an inducement for reclamation, all future inhabitants of the city and its environs were to be free and secure in their lives and property. They would be judged "according to the laws, customs, and decrees" set out by the first great archbishop of a restored Tarragona, Olaguer. The task of establishing such a legal infrastructure was a slow one; in 1129, the prelate, in conjunction with a Norman mercenary, Robert Burdet, who was granted half of the urban jurisdiction, promised that all city residents of Tarragona would be judged "according to the laws and good customs" that he would decree in conjunction with the town council. The optimum phrase of this document for understanding the subsequent growth of the *Usatges* was that which assured Tarragona settlers that they would "be neither judged nor punished" except by the statutes decreed for their city.[90] Despite these assurances, the promised municipal laws were not fully forthcoming and, in the reign of Ramón Berenguer IV, the city was touched by general legislation originating from the Barcelona court. With the accession in 1148 of the next archbishop, Bernat de Tort, Robert Burdet, who also bore the title Prince of Tarragona, formally pledged to carry out the terms of all prior agreements concluded with Olaguer. Instead of upholding the rendering of

88. Udina Martorell and Udina i Abelló, "Consideracions," 96.
89. *Marca*, doc. 310, p. 1192; Balari, *Orígenes históricos de Cataluña*, 2: 491.
90. *Marca*, docs. 358, 373, pp. 1247, 1252; Font Rius, *Cartas*, 1: docs. 49, 51, pp. 83, 88; Bastardas, *La problematica de Usatges*, 38.

justice in line with the city's own laws, Robert swore that all suits in the city would be adjudicated by "the laws and customs of the Barcelona court."[91] When the archbishop reciprocated in stating an official relationship with the Prince of Tarragona, he used much the same phraseology.[92] Up to this point, the "court usages" and "court rules" of the Count of Barcelona were little more than technical guidelines for the adjudication of suits before the *curia comitis*. Now, with no steady line of precedence, the "good customs" of the Barcelona court were well enough known to be adopted by two public figures for the jurisdiction they shared. As Bastardas suggests, the only plausible explanation is that the *Usatges of Barcelona* had entered into some type of written format which was officially accepted by 1148 as the legal norm of the Count of Barcelona's court and, as such, the law of the lands over which he exercised authority.[93]

The indication of a written set of court usages demonstrable from the Tarragona documents of 1148–49 is reinforced by the testimony of the next five decades. When Ramón Berenguer IV entered into litigation in 1151 with one of his retainers, Galceran de Sals, their disputes were adjudicated "legally and customarily" (*legaliter et usualiter*). The customary law on which the judges of the panel based their verdicts was, in fact, "a written law of custom" (*lex usuaria*). From the seven exact citations preserved in the proceedings of 1151, this law was none other than the *Usatges of Barcelona*.[94] In a suit of 1157 with another of his court barons Pere de Puigvert, the count again based his defense on portions of the new code which are referred to as the "customs of the Barcelona court" (*mores Barchinonensis curie*). Again, it is clear that these customs refer to the *Usatges* from the number of verbatim passages included within the tribunal's verdict.[95] In the decades which followed, the *Usatges* retained their adjudicative importance, even when the count was not a disputant. In 1160 when the monastery of San Cugat de Valles sued a neighboring noble over title to castle lands, the "legitimate possession" of the property in question was determined "according to the law and the customs of the court of Barcelona."[96] When the same monastery in the same year disputed with one of its castellans over the

---

91. Font Rius, *Cartas*, 1: doc. 66, p. 108; Bastardas, *La problematica de Usatges*, 38.

92. *Marca*, doc. 406, p. 1302; Font Rius, *Cartas*, 1: doc. 69, p. 113; Bastardas, *La problematica de Usatges*, 38.

93. Bastardas, *La problematica de Usatges*, 38.

94. Appendix II, no. V; *CDACA* 4: doc. 146, pp. 343–46; *LFM* 2: doc. 511, pp. 24–26; Bastardas, *La problematica de Usatges*, 40–43; Aquilino Iglesia Ferreirós, "La creación del derecho en Cataluña," *AHDE* 47(1977): 275; Balari, *Origines históricos de Cataluña*, 2: 491.

95. *LFM* 1: doc. 253, pp. 269–73; Balari, *Origenes históricos de Cataluña*, 2: 492.

96. *CSCV* 3: doc. 1036, pp. 205–6.

control of the castle he held, the functionary made clear reference to one of the *Usatges* articles when he claimed that this custody had to be returned to him within ten days "just as it had been decreed in the Barcelona court."[97]

If the *Usatges* had only been used for adjudication of suits, their spread as a true *leges patriae* would not have been accomplished as quickly as it was or it might have even been retarded completely.[98] A number of factors, however, impelled the acceptance of the *Usatges* as the base law for most of the Catalan territory controlled by the Count. At the heart of this transformation stood a formal comital act of legislation which was secured in writing. Though always a remarkably literate environment, the comital court placed an increased emphasis on the written record from the reign of Alfonso II. Important matters including verdicts, feudal pacts, and land sales or transfers were increasingly "committed to writing so [they] should not slip from memory to the rust of oblivion"[99] and "so one may lay claim to this reference whenever doubt arises."[100] The upshot of such careful record keeping and accountability was the emergence of true administrative organs within the court from the era of Alfonso II.[101] At the forefront of this movement was the issuance of the *Usatges* in a written form. Though variants in the copies of the code surely existed in these first years of its graphic life, it attained a currency never possible when merely a set of judicial precedents retained in the memory or casebook of a small number of judges.

The establishment of the "court usages" in a written format was only one step toward the expanded sovereignty of the count of Barcelona. It is hardly unusual, then, that the count and his officials encouraged the prestige of the code by its continued judicial use and increasing influence on legislation.[102] As Alfonso issued foral laws for individual urban settlements, he was careful to either extend practices outlined in the *Usatges* into the municipal laws or declare that the code in full would act as an adjunct for

97. ACA, Pergaminos de Ramón Berenguer IV, no. 342; Balari, *Origines históricos de Cataluña*, 2: 492.

98. Font Rius, *Cartas*, 1: doc. 122, p. 178; Iglesia Ferreirós, "La creación," 257.

99. *LFM* 1: doc. 225, p. 234; Iglesia Ferreirós, "La creación," 270. Compare with Socrates' view on the deleterious effects of writing which leds men away from the "exercise of memory because they rely on what is written" (cited in Clanchy, *From Memory to Written Record*, 253).

100. Iglesia Ferreiros, "La creación," 262.

101. Bisson, *Medieval Crown*, 49.

102. For relationship of royal legislation amd sovereignty, see Wolf, "Gesetzgebung und Kodifikationen," 160–62; John Michael Wallace-Hadrill, *Early Germanic Kingship in England and on the Continent* (Oxford: Clarendon Press, 1971), 149; Wormald, "*Lex Scripta* and *Verbum Regis*," 138.

the enforcement of law in the towns.[103] On a broader scale, the *Usatges* were bound to the only true source of written, territorial law in the Count of Barcelona's lands — the *pax et treuga*. As Alfonso turned to the long-unused peace and truce and refashioned it as an administrative tool, he was careful to define its relationship with the *Usatges*. In the first of the sovereign's territorial peaces, that of Fondarella in 1173, the "written custom" (*consuetudinem scriptum*) plays an important role in defining general feudal norms and then attaching them to the peace and truce. Thus the article of the code which dealt with a vassal's treason against a lord was bolstered by calling for the ejection of the traitor from the protection of the peace.[104] Despite the archaic tone of the Fondarella peace, the Catalan barony saw it as a threat to several articles of the *Usatges* and raised these objections when Alfonso convened an assembly at Gerona in 1188 to promulgate another set of peace statutes. Surrendering to the will of his great men, Alfonso reformulated the affiliation of the *pax et treuga* and the "written usage" (*scriptum usaticum*) on several points. Passages from the code which dealt with the murder or injury of the comital bailiffs, the mortgaging of the possessions of such officials, and terms of castle tenure and surrender by castellans and lords were incorporated fully into the peace. The most significant article of the Gerona assembly was that which made violation of any part of the *Usatges* an infraction of the peace and truce. Violators of the code could thus be ejected from the protection of the peace and attacked with impunity.[105] Despite Alfonso's efforts to assure the Catalan barons that the peace statutes would not challenge the full jurisdictional base of the *Usatges*, they remained unconvinced, especially when he convened yet another assembly at Barcelona in 1192 for the express purpose of promulgating a "constitution of new peaces." Though the barons initially acquiesced to the will of their sovereign as legislator, their fear of legal innovations that might put the *Usatges* at risk quickly surfaced. Thus, "at their earnest request and pressure," Alfonso angrily gave in and issued a proclamation from Barbastro which declared that all Catalan peace and truces prior to 1192, "which the very written law of the *Usatges* clearly proclaims," would remain forever in force.[106] It is significant that in the midst of a dispute between sovereign and nobility which would be reenacted time and again for the next two hundred years, the *Usatges* would serve as a guarantor of privileged position

---

103. Font Rius, *Cartas*, 1: docs. 122, 149, pp. 176–78, 208–10.
104. *Marca*, art. 15, p. 1365; Bisson, *Medieval Crown*, 49–50.
105. *CAVC* I, pt. 1: arts. 7, 8, 14, 15, pp. 66–67; Bisson, *Medieval Crown*, 52–53.
106. *CAVC* I, pt. 1: 62; Bisson, *Medieval Crown*, 53.

for both sides. Ruler and subject alike could appeal to and defend the same law, which from its heterogeneous nature gave something of great worth to each. As a result of its expanded acceptance on all levels, the code constituted a territorial standard of law within Catalonia and, to some extent, throughout Provence. Indeed, the rise of the "fuero and custom of Catalonia" was widespread enough in Provence to guarantee the preservation of a "volume of the Barcelona laws" (*volumen legum barchinonensium*) in one of the region's clerical libraries before the end of twelfth century.[107]

Assessment of a Law Code

At the center of all the controversies the *Usatges* have engendered lies the code itself. At once an enigma and a mine of information that varies greatly in quality, the textual record of the code itself provides some of the most significant clues about its evolution.

The first assertion that can be drawn from the code focuses on the complexities of its early existence. If only the first three articles of the *Usatges* had survived, one would have to assume that it was a unified law code promulgated by Ramón Berenguer I and his third wife Almodis before a group of "magnates of the land." As these first articles proclaim, the reason for such a massive legislative undertaking was a straightforward one: the *Liber Judiciorum* was no longer universally applicable to all legal situations of the Spanish March, and so the count, basing his lawmaking on certain passages of Visigothic law, acted to fill in the gaps of the old written law with judicial precedents based on the region's customary law. Although not a good indicator of the code's exact date, the prologue of the *Usatges* is still a significant starting point for the study of the laws. Certain portions of the opening section refute the possibility of a single legislative origin for the code. Ramón Berenguer I is referred to as "the Old" (*vetus*), a sobriquet not applied to the count until the reign of his great-grandson Ramón Berenguer IV. An earlier variant of the same nickname, *vetulus*, was first cited in 1092.[108] The list of great men who supposedly witnessed the decree of the *Usatges* is also a flawed one. All the nobles mentioned had served in Ramón Berenguer I's court at one time or another but the vast disparity in their

107. Gerard Giordanengo, "Vocabulaire et formulaires féodaux en Provence et en Dauphine (XIIe–XIVe siècles)," *Structures féodales*, 89–90; For the formation of Provençal written law of era, see André Gouron, "Gênes et le Droit Provençal," in Gouron, *Études*, 7–15.
108. Balari, *Origines historicos de Cataluña*, 2: 451–52.

ages makes their attendance at the same assembly highly unlikely. Two cases are instructive. The great legist Guillem March seems to have ended his career as comital judge as Ramón Berenguer was commencing his reign in 1035.[109] Guillem Ramón [I] de Montcada, on the other hand, received his title as seneschal from 1068, but remained an important member of the comital court through three succeeding reigns and only ended his service at his death in 1120.[110] Despite its inaccuracies and inconsistencies, the prologue of the *Usatges* is eloquent on several points. The author of this introduction, though perhaps not even alive in the time of Ramón Berenguer "the Old," still had access to documents of this earlier era and a bank of traditions transmuted through curial channels. The reason he gives for the promulgation of the code accurately reflects the count of Barcelona's need for a judicative adaptation in the mid-eleventh century. Like so much of the code it introduces, then, the prologue seems either a mixture of eleventh- and twelfth-century elements or a conscious twelfth-century attempt to cast its work in the idiom of a much earlier era. In either case, the last legist who turned his hand to the *Usatges* project felt impelled to reinforce its validity by highlighting the code with a lengthy history of application and use.

As one of the first editors of the *Usatges* in the twentieth century, Ramón d'Abadal i de Vinyals, has observed, the code is "an aggregate of legal texts of different epochs and varied sources."[111] These legal strata can be seen within ranges of articles and in individual articles themselves. Since such internal evidence is open to various interpretations, three major lines of chronological classification have been based on the clues the *Usatges* provide: the linguistic, structural, and comparative approaches. Following the linguistic method, around the end of the nineteenth century, such scholars as José Balari Jovany and Guillermo María de Broca y Montagut investigated the style and syntax of the code to determine which of its articles were original and which were later accretions. Passages in the first group read as if copied directly from eleventh-century decrees, with verbs in the initial clause cast in the present indicative plural. In passages in the second group, a narrator intrudes and the initial verbs are expressed in the past indicative plural. By using such simple linguistic indicators, scholars of the *Usatges* hoped to delineate the various stages of the code's growth.

---

109. Balari, *Orígines históricos de Cataluña*, 2: 407, 411–14, 471–80; Valls-Taberner, "El liber iudicum popularis," *Obras*, 2: 245–46.

110. John C. Shideler, *A Medieval Catalan Noble Family: The Montcadas, 1000–1230* (Berkeley: University of California Press, 1984), 18–20, 24–35; Sobreques, *Els Barons*, 48–49.

111. *Usatges de Barcelona*, ed. d'Abadal i de Vinyals and Valls Taberner, xi.

In the second means of code chronology, the focus of scholarly investigation was the accumulation of later materials in the *Usatges*. This added material, the work of later commentators and copyists, is not consistent with an eleventh-century environment.[112] Though they shared some methodological bases with the earlier linguistic investigators of the *Usatges*, such twentieth-century investigators as Felipe Mateu i Llopis and Pierre Bonnassie focused not on language but rather on the code's structural elements to at least partially determine which of the code's articles have an eleventh-century vintage. The principal indicator of such a textual baserock for Mateu i Llopis and Bonnassie was the mention in the code's articles of coins known to be in circulation throughout Christian and Muslim Spain in the eleventh-century. For the practitioners of this second type of textual archaeology, the citation of so many different types of coinage in the body of the *Usatges* could only mean that the laws came into being during a long period during the mid-eleventh century.[113] The culmination of the first two methods used to give the *Usatges* a verifiable date was the work of Ferran Valls i Taberner. This editor of the code in 1913 spent much of the next two decades in using the research of earlier scholars to posit the thoery that the *Usatges* came into being in certain phases during Ramón Berenguer I's reign.[114]

In the most recent venue of study, which focused on the connections among the code's parts, such authorities as Guido Carlo Mor and Joan Bastardas have attempted to understand the whole by comparing all the earliest copies of the *Usatges* in Latin and Catalan to see which articles constituted an original version and which were later additions or glosses. From this comparison of editions, Mor and Bastardas concluded that the *Usatges* had indeed evolved in stages. But rather than being a few years long, they declared that these stages bridged much of the later eleventh and twelfth centuries.[115]

None of these approaches are entirely satisfactory, since in one way or another they portray the *Usatges* as a germ of original laws surrounded by layer after layer of supplementary material. This view is entirely too simplistic. Original, eleventh-century and secondary, twelfth-century elements clearly existed in the written code which emerged after 1149, but they may

112. Balari, *Origenes históricos de Cataluña*, 2: 494; Broca y Montagut, *Historia del derecho*, 141–67.
113. Felipe Mateu i Llopis, "El '*aureum valencie*' en los '*usatici barchinone*': Estudios de las Usatges," *Numisma* 6(1956): 12–27; Bonnassie, *La Catalogne*, 2: 722–8.
114. See note 218.
115. Mor, "La formación del texto," 412–59; Bastardas i Parera, *La problematica de Usatges*, 13–28.

not have played a part in the primitive "court usages" which came into use in Barcelona tribunals from the reign of Ramón Berenguer I. Though a common set of *usatici* must have existed in the broadest sense, they were not passed from one generation of judges to the next unchanged. The variants undoubtedly made their way into the earliest compilations and even after the laws reached a more polished and rectified form, the anomalies of their early existence were preserved. Thus we see a number of sections in the code addressing the same problems but in somewhat different ways.

The most striking of these variants focus on penalties for murder and assault. In the first and presumably some of the oldest of the *Usatges* articles (4–11), a schedule of fines for violent crime is arranged in accordance with the status of the victim and the seriousness of the offense. While this set of penalties is rooted in Visigothic law, it seems to share much with the wergeld of the barbarian codes.[116] Since these fines were payable in the gold coinage of Ramón Berenguer I and his sons, it seems likely they have a late eleventh-century pedigree. Another set of fines are also included in the code (articles 11–17). Though treating with the same kind of violent crime, the victims were to be compensated with types of silver coinage that circulated in the lands of the count of Barcelona throughout the eleventh and twelfth century.[117] The different approaches of these two sections to the malefactor points to different authors working in distinct eras. In the "golden" articles, the victim's place in society determined the amercement, while in the "silver" articles the emendations were assessed solely according to the seriousness of the crime.

The inclusion of such similar and different statutes within the same corpus of law reveals something of how that corpus developed as an entity. Rather than growing from a small core out to a great but regularly defined periphery, the earliest form of the *Usatges* in their earliest form were rather a cluster of customary legal amoebas that slowly fused into even greater legal cells. Homogeneity was not always the result of such amalgamation. Anomalous approaches to the same problems might exist side by side since they all had the validating mark of being custom. The *Usatges* in their written form is thus not one code but a number of compilations linked together — sometimes successfully, sometimes less so — by passages of an explanatory

---

116. Julius Goebel, *Felony and Misdemeanor: A Study in the History of Criminal Law* (New York: The Commonwealth Fund, 1938; Philadelphia: University of Pennsylvania Press, 1976), 7, n.8; *Laws of the Alamans and Bavarians*, trans. Theodore John Rivers (Philadelphia: University of Pennsylvania Press, 1977), 50, 85–91.

117. Mateu i Llopis, "El '*Aureum Valencie*'" 26–27.

nature. The author of these passages, who served as interlocutor for all other judges and legists involved in the long process of turning Barcelona usage into law, was not merely the final editor but also "a historian whose work was the fruit of his researches."[118] In spite of the unifying hand of its last editor, the earlier groupings of "court usages" could not be fused out of existence even in the name of textual efficiency. Since the "fundamental base" of the *Usatges* was an evolving set of curial precedents that stood as an adjunct to the *Liber Judiciorum*, it thus shared the inviolability and unchangeability of Visigothic law.[119] A number of usage strains, which might have been defined in judgments rendered by the count of Barcelona's tribunals, surely passed through several compilations that may have existed contemporaneously and then fed into the first official written version of the code.[120] The illogicalities of the code are the logical result. Only by a thoroughgoing examination, assessment, and recasting of the different sets of "court usages" could a more systematic legal statement have been attained. Yet such "innovations" might have blocked acceptance of the laws on a wide scale. As it was, great changes had been appended to the "court usages," which transformed them from simple proclamations of customary law to a clearsighted statement of sovereignty for the count of Barcelona.

Law of Prince, Law of Ruler

Regardless of the uncertainties of the *Usatges* before they left the path of custom and entered on the high road of written law, the code's importance in Catalan life was quickly shown when both ruler and ruled claimed it as their own. The success of the laws in this regard must be attributed to the skillful weaving of comital assertions of public power with the acknowledged rights and duties of lords and vassals. The result was, in Thomas Bisson's words, a "grafting a custom of fiefs onto Roman-Visigothic principles of public order."[121] With this in mind, the most efficient treatment of the jumbled mass of incongruities that comprise the *Usatges* is afforded by a focus on the code as a statement of the count of Barcelona's power and a legal ordering of Catalan society under the aegis of the same count's proclaimed authority.

118. Bastardas, *La problematica de Usatges*, 33.
119. *Usatges*, ed. d'Abadal i de Vinyals and Valls Taberner, xv.
120. Bastardas, *La problematica de Usatges*, 44–49, Udina Martorell and Udina i Abelló, "Consideracions," 95–96.
121. Bisson, "Problem," 466.

Like all successful non-royal rulers to emerge from the ruins of the Carolingian empire, the count of Barcelona insisted he had kinglike authority while never assuming a royal title. The thirteenth-century chronicler Bernat Desclot fabricated the following speech for Ramón Berenguer IV to explain the lack of a kingship in Catalonia:

> While I live I will not be called king. I am now one of the better counts of the world and if I were called king, I would certainly not be one of the best.[122]

Though fictional, this statement demonstrates with some clarity that ruling without a royal title could only be carried out from a secure base of authority. This foundation of ruling validity was brought about by the "intitulation" (*intitulatio*) of the non-royal ruler with political and ethical attributes.[123] For the count of Barcelona, this development had effectively begun with Wifred I and reached its culmination with the *Usatges*. Interestingly, with the full inheritance of a royal title for Aragon by Alfonso II in 1162, the rulers of Catalonia felt less anxious about their claims to power and the terms of their intitulation were less and less used.[124]

Besides his titles of count, duke, and marquis, the most defensible aspect of sovereignty claimed by the ruler of Barcelona was that attached to the term *potestas*. In the framework of Roman law, the word signified the right to dispose of property or the extensive control which the head of household or *paterfamilias* held over its members or the extensive power a master exercised over a slave. In Roman political terms, *potestas* was often equated with *imperium*, the broad mandate the greatest magistrates possessed in order to carry out their duties.[125] By the early Middle Ages, the term referred as much to the office as to the officeholder. In Carolingian political environment, a *potestas* was a "public person" or official with a broadly defined authority to rule sizeable territories in the name of the Emperor.[126] In feudal terms, the word came to mean the invested jurisdiction or control possessed by a castellan or vassal over a castle or fief which had to be returned to the "eminent lord" whenever he requested it.[127] Though the term could signify a suzerain, the count of Barcelona did not

---

122. d'Abadal y de Vinyals, "Vida politica," xlvii.

123. Henry A. Myers, *Medieval Kingship: The Origins and Development of Western Monarchy in All Stages from the Fall of Rome to the Fifteenth Century* (Chicago: Nelson-Hall, 1972), 111–14.

124. Udina Martorell and Udina i Abelló, "Consideracions," 94.

125. Balari, *Origenes Históricos* 2:497; Francisco Hernández Tejero, "Sobre el concepto de *'potestas*,'" *AHDE* 17(1946): 605–24.

126. Bonnassie, *La Catalogne*, 1: 136–38; Rodón Binué, *El lenguaje técnico*, 202.

127. Rodón Binué, *El lenguaje técnico*, 200–201; Valdeavellano, *Historia de las instituciónes*, 399–400.

base his own authority on a position of overlordship but tied it firmly to the delegation of jurisdiction by Charlemagne and his successors. Dominance over all the counties of the old Spanish March could hardly be claimed by the count of Barcelona, since several other counts, descendants of Wifred I's brothers, also considered themselves *potestates*.[128] The ascendance of the count of Barcelona could thus not be bound to the competence of any office but rather to the political idea that he was the best fitted to rule. As the fifteenth-century commentator on the *Usatges*, Jaume de Montjuich, observed:

> All the counts of Catalonia were equal with the counts of Barcelona but because of the injustice of the land they conceded that the count of Barcelona was made more powerful and just than the others.[129]

At the center of the count's claim to such a extensive authority was the title *princeps*. Just as the *Usatges* were the result of a complicated process of legal evolution, the term "prince" itself had followed a long and tortuous road. It had a long military and constitutional history in Republic and Empire alike.[130] In the period after Carolingian power had waned in the Spanish March, the greatest remaining indigenous authorities in the region, the counts and viscounts, were known as *principes*. The count of Barcelona in particular utilized the title and all the authority it implied throughout the eleventh century.[131] In the rebellion of Mir Geribert and Ramón Berenguer I's drive to suppress it, the claim to princely status was a significant weapon. Mir's pretension to the title *princeps Olerdulae* was met by the strong counter claim from the count for a broader supremacy in the "principate of his land."[132] This title was also one conferred anew along with feudal grants and posts of even more significance, as with Robert Burdet, who became the "Prince of Tarragona" in 1128, and Ramón Berenguer IV who, with his marriage to Petronilla, acceded to power in Aragón in 1137 but never bore a regal title there, being known instead as the *princeps Aragonensium*.[133] As the count of Barcelona's power grew during the twelfth century, the title of *princeps* began to symbolize his

---

128. Bonnassie, *La Catalogne*, 1: 128.

129. Guillermo Maria Broca y Montagut, "Traça de classificació del *Usatges* y idea de la *potestat*," *Anuari* 1 (1907): 283–84.

130. Arnold Hugh Martin Jones, *Augustus* (London: Chatto and Windus, 1970; New York: W. W. Norton, 1971), 83; Lily Ross Taylor, *Party Politics in the Age of Caesar* (Berkeley: University of California Press, 1961; reprint, 1971), 91.

131. Lewis, *Development*, 227, 348–49; Balari, *Orígenes históricos*, 2: 441.

132. *Marca*, doc. 248, p. 1113; Bonnassie, *La Catalogne*, 2: 628.

133. Lewis, *Development*, 354–55, 373–75; *Marca*, doc. 373, pp. 1261–63; Bofarull y Moscaró, *Los condes*, 2: 183–85.

ambition for an ever broader horizon of sovereignty over Catalonia. This desire was shaped and reshaped in the half century after it was first stated in the *Usatges* until it became an effective doctrine of kingship that supported the count's repeated assertions to sovereignty and validated his actions on behalf of the public weal. Though a "political ideal" — to use Udina Martorell's words —, the concept of *princeps* provided a diagram for ruling to which each of Ramón Berenguer I's successors added detail. Thus by the era of Pedro II, it was widely asserted and accepted in comital circles that

> kings and princes of the land are to be useful to those subject to them, to love and cherish these people in many ways, to govern them with complete care in righteousness and justice and to entirely remove from them every oppression and grievance whatsoever.[134]

While the titles *princeps* and *potestas* represented two distinct aspects of the count of Barcelona's authority, they came to be used interchangeably in the *Usatges*, and this fact, according to d'Abadal i de Vinyals, is one of the major causes for the "characteristic imprecision" of the code. The confusion between the aspects of power represented by the two terms increased by their long period of evolution and mutual influence. The final compilers of the *Usatges* aided in the virtual merging of the two words into a single statement of political superiority for the count of Barcelona by indiscriminately applying "Roman legal qualifications" to both concepts.[135] The princely and potestative functions now became a single reservoir of self-proclaimed authority which the Barcelona ruler could draw on to nourish his claims to sovereignty.

The regalist articles of the *Usatges*, though with some roots in Catalonia's customary legal past, were, as Balari suggests, largely a "spontaneous manifestation of the sovereign's will."[136] The only certifiable link to a longstanding legislative comital tradition was the peace and truce. This restricted role of eleventh-century pacification which the count shared with the bishops of Catalonia was amplified by the code in a way reminiscent of Visigothic and Frankish models.[137] Thus the count of Barcelona's role as protector of the "helpless" was combined with a more general "protection" (*emperamentum*). As a result, the count as *princeps* was responsible for the

---

134. ACA, Pergaminos de Pedro II, no. 298; *CDACA*, 4: doc. 38, p. 102.
135. d'Abadal i de Vinyals, "La vida politica," xlix; Udina Martorell and Udina i Abelló, "Consideracions," 92.
136. Balari, *Orígenes históricos*, 2: 496.
137. Bisson, "Problem," 467.

"peace and security" of all his lands. Within this ambit of authority, the prince took as an obligation of his office and position the protection of all shipping coming to or leaving Barcelona, the region's canal network, and coinage.[138] As *potestas* or ruler, the count formally offered his protection to any persons including his officials on route to or from the comital court as well as to lords illegally attacked by vassals and vice versa.[139] The amalgamation of feudal and non-feudal protection was thus attached to the person of the count, who himself represented the transmutation of prince and ruler into sovereign.[140]

Along with the protective role outlined in the *Usatges*, the position of judge was also firmly reinforced for the count of Barcelona. In feudal terms, the count, like any lord, settled the disputes of his vassals, and like any suzerain, was the final arbiter of grievances between other lords and their vassals. The focal point of the count's adjudicative activities in both feudal and non-feudal matters was the *curia comitis*. Verdicts rendered by a panel of judges appointed from the count's retainers was reinforced "by the approval and judgement" of the whole court. The acceptance of such sentences by the litigants and the land at large was considered crucial by the authors of the *Usatges* because whoever refused "the judgment of the court" was a madman who attacked its very "veracity" and that of the ruler himself.[141] The count was also given a judicial, or more properly a punitive, role outside the court in carrying out corporal punishment for certain criminal acts including murder, theft, robbery, adultery, assault, and sorcery.[142] He was also given the sole responsibility for rendering judgments concerning situations not covered in customary or Visigothic law. Interestingly, such "royal discretion" set judicial precedent which eventually passed into written, territorial law — the very process that had brought the *Usatges* themselves into being.[143] The judicial powers attributed to the count of Barcelona by the *Usatges* were also another base of his sovereignty. Very much like Visigothic and Carolingian rulers before him, the count was placed at the apex of the civil judicature and made the only authority to punish infamous or criminal acts.

The last stage of sovereignty expansion the *Usatges* proclaimed for the

138. *Usatges*, arts. 57, 58, 60, 62, 69, pp. 92, 94, 96, 98, 106.
139. *Usatges*, arts. 41, 59, 61, 67, pp. 82, 94, 98, 104.
140. *Usatges*, arts. 64, 99, pp. 102, 134.
141. *Usatges*, arts. 40, 42, 122, pp. 82, 84, 156.
142. *Usatges*, art. 2, p. 50.
143. *LV* VII, 1, 4, p. 336.

count of Barcelona centered on the extent of his public prerogatives. The laws openly and firmly declared that roads, highways, rivers, springs, pastureland, forests, crags, and other defensible sites were under the jurisdiction of the count who held them for the realm at large.[144] Though there was some basis for such comital claims, the assertion that only he had power over various types of lands mentioned in the code ran counter to the realities of land settlement since the time of the Spanish March. In allodial transfers and feudal grants from the tenth century onward, possession or custody of the types of land restricted to the count, were freely granted in every stratum of Catalan society without reference to comital authority.[145] Even the comital involvement in the peace and truce did little until the late twelfth century to further regalian rights over such "public" features of the Catalan landscape as the major road network.[146] The most successfully implemented of the count's claims based on *potestas* was that which restricted the building of any structure on high ground or the use of any type of siege equipment without the count's permission.[147]

The princely ideal of the count of Barcelona is best expressed in the code's articles which focus on a sovereignty emanating from the *curia comitis*. All the prerogatives he claimed for himself in his realm came to light in microcosm within the circle of his court. It was consistent with his princely honor to maintain a "great household" (*magna familia*) around him as both a stage for his ruling pretensions and a means of sharing the aura of his power with the great men of his lands. These retainers were to be fed and clothed in a lavish way as long as they sojourned with the monarch. While the sovereign's drive for a fully-accepted basis of power and authority emanated from the self-conscious grandeur of his court, his validity as ruler was bound to the righteousness of his character. Thus, since many a realm had been ruined "by an evil prince who is without either truth or justice," the ruler was bound by his office to maintain a "sincere and perfect faith" as well as "truthful speech."[148]

The difference between the state of attributed power or the possession of qualities which certified the right to such power and that actually held by

144. *Usatges*, arts. 59, 68, 69, pp. 94, 106; Marc Bloch, *French Rural History: An Essay on Basic Characteristics*, trans. Janet Sondheimer (1931; reprint Berkeley: University of California Press, 1966), 183.
145. *CSCV* 1: doc. 2, p. 50.
146. *LFM* 2: doc. 735, pp. 243–44; *CAVC*, I, pt. 1, pp. 67, 69, 73–74, 82.
147. *Usatges*, art. 73, pp. 110–12; *LFM* 2: docs. 511, 798, pp. 24, 283; *CDACA* 4: docs 23, 146, pp. 55–56, 344.
148. *Usatges*, arts. 60, 103, pp. 96, 136–38.

the count of Barcelona demonstrates with some clarity what the principal articles of the *Usatges* intend. From a real but often ill-defined foundation of authority, the count was endowed by the sanction of written law with a much richer language of dominion, which he learned to speak with growing fluency as the twelfth century ended.

Law of Lords, Law of Vassals

The *Usatges* justified its own existence in most primal terms: the Visigothic "Book of Judges" contained no section on feudal relations for judges to turn to in making their decisions and thus a new law was needed to address new social situations. The inapplicability of law codes of late antiquity to the evolving realities of feudalism was not unique to Catalonia but occurred in all the lands of the defunct Carolingian empire. After a period of legal gestation and adaptation in the tenth century, feudal practice was slowly "integrated" into systems of law in the eleventh and twelfth centuries. The legal implications of feudal bonds were addressed in urban statutes and imperial decrees. The most important of these legislative acts were imperial edicts which defined the rights and duties of lords and vassals. In 1037 at Milan, Emperor Conrad II (1024–39) laid out the legal framework in which Italian lords and vassals were to operate.[149] In 1158 at Roncaglia, Emperor Frederick I Barbarossa (1152–90) formally unified the network of feudal relations under the aegis of his imperial power. In the latter set of edicts, the influence of Roman law is clearly discernible as disparate feudal practices were systematized and the power of the Emperor was proclaimed to supersede all the feudatories of his Italian lands.[150] Even before Roncaglia, however, the new trends of Roman jurisprudence had turned to the welter of feudal practice and attempted to make some legal sense of it in such books as the *Libri Feudorum* of Umberto de Orto which became a standard textbook at Bologna from the mid-twelfth century. In this political and academic milieu, the *Usatges* came into being. The influence of Roman law on the code's authors is easily demonstrable. Yet in the feudal articles of their work, they did not attempt to fashion a full comital suzerainty but rather aimed at forming a general custom which, as Bisson says, was "applicable to all lords, vassals, and fiefs."[151]

149. *History of Feudalism*, doc. 2, pp. 107–9.
150. *History of Feudalism*, doc. 38, pp. 237–39.
151. Bisson, "Problem," 467.

The main thrust of the feudal articles of the *Usatges* was an ordering of the myriad bonds which tied lords to vassals in Catalonia. The relations delineated in the code accurately reflect the terms of the pacts which proliferated during the reign of Ramón Berenguer "the Old."[152] Homage and fealty were so commonplace that they did not warrant lengthy description. As the delineation of a "hierarchy of commended men," the *Usatges* were much more concerned with practice than with theory.[153] They sought to lay out tenurial, judicial, and military standards common to all feudal relationships in the areas of Catalonia controlled by the count of Barcelona. Multiple feudal lords were discussed in ideal and real terms. Liege homage was defined at the simplest level: a liege vassal would theoretically have only one liege lord whom he promised to serve above all others. The code also reflects the real world of Catalan feudalism, since it allowed vassals to have more than one liege lord under certain conditions.[154] Regardless of the number of lords and vassals a person might have, it was the conditions of service or protection that most interested the authors of the *Usatges*.

Vassalic dues and rights as they appear in the *Usatges* are much the same as as in the eleventh-century *convenientia*. Vassals held the custody of their fiefs or castles conditionally—they could not alienate their tenure without their lord's consent.[155] The services owed by vassals to lords were both military and legal. As the bulk of his temporary seigneurial army, vassalic "aid" (*iuvamen*) included defense of the lord on the battlefield and ransoming him if captured.[156] As "natural trustees of their lords," vassals could be required to "post sureties" (*firmare directum*) and "guaranties" (*pignora, plivios*) for their lords involved in litigation.[157] The rights a vassal could claim from the *Usatges* were few but significant. If a lord asked anything beyond the conventional terms that tied him to his man, the vassal could demand larger fiefs to support this greater level of service.[158] The

---

152. Bonnassie, *La Catalogne*, 2: 780.

153. Bisson, "Feudalism," 185.

154. *Usatges*, arts. 5, 20, 26, 33, 35, 72, 123, pp. 56, 66, 78, 110, 123; Bonnassie, *La Catalogne*, 2: 743–45; Bonnassie, *Slavery*, 172–78, 187; Pierre Bonnassie, "Les conventions féodales dans la Catalogne du XIe siècle," *Les structures sociales de l'Aquitaine, du Languedoc et de l'Espagne au premier âge féodal* (Paris: Éditions du CNRS, 1969), 97–99, 208.

155. *Usatges*, arts. 26, 39, pp. 72, 82.

156. *Usatges*, arts. 28–31, 34, pp. 74–76, 78; Bonnassie, *La Catalogne*, 2: 748, 767–68; Thomas N. Bisson, "The Military Origins of Military Representation," *AHR* 71 (1966): 1203.

157. *Usatges*, arts. 20, 24, 35, 38, 113, 118, 125, pp. 66, 70, 78, 146, 160; Bonnassie, *La Catalogne*, 2: 768–71.

158. *Usatges*, arts. 32, C6, pp. 76, 172.

custody of fortresses redeemed by lords had to be given back to their men within a defined period — normally ten days.[159] As members of seigneurial hosts, vassals could demand reimbursement of personal losses suffered on active duty.[160] The most significant right bestowed on vassals by the *Usatges* was the establishment of the count of Barcelona as protector of men unjustly punished or deprived of their fiefs by their lords.[161]

The code's treatment of the lord's part of the feudal bargain concentrates almost completely on seigneurial rights over vassals. Lords had the same obligations to their men as did the count of Barcelona to his vassals; that is, "to grant redress, render justice, support the oppressed, and come to the aid of the besieged."[162] What a lord could expect from a vassal was much more carefully defined in the code. The lord granted a fief in expectation of prescribed services from his vassal. If the vassal defaulted in any of these duties, the lord could confiscate the fief and retain it until the required service was carried out.[163] Though fiefs in Catalonia were becoming heritable by the mid-twelfth century, a lord was allowed by the *Usatges* to grant the fief of a deceased, childless vassal to whomever he wished or to decide which child of an intestate vassal should accede to the paternal fief.[164] A number of lordly rights discussed in the code were even more extensive. By the *exorquia*, the lord could claim a portion of a deceased vassal's estate if no heirs survived him. By the *intestia*, the lord could gain a similar portion of a vassalic estate provided no will had been left. By the *cugucia*, a lord had rights to a part of the property of his vassal's wife who was a proven adulteress.[165] Though these rules would provide a basis for lordly dominance of the peasantry in Catalonia in centuries to come, the overall focus of the *Usatges* on lord-vassal relations was well within the pragmatic limits of the *convenientia*, which counseled a lord "not to demand more from his vassal than he could give."[166]

The *Usatges* spent as much detail on the dispute which could break master from man as they did on the connections of service which linked

159. *Usatges*, arts. 26, 39, pp. 72, 82.
160. *Usatges*, art. 30, p. 76.
161. *Usatges*, art. 41, p. 82.
162. *Usatges*, art. 103, p. 138; Bonnassie, *La Catalogne*, 2: 772.
163. *Usatges*, art. 30. p. 76.
164. *Usatges*, arts. 27, 121, pp. 74, 156; Bonnassie, *La Catalogne*, 2: 763–64.
165. *Usatges*, arts. 65, 86, 117, pp. 102, 122, 124, 150; Bonnassie, *La Catalogne*, 2: 827–28; Bonnassie, *Slavery*, 237–38; Paul Freedman, "The Enserfment Process in Medieval Catalonia," *Viator* 13(1982): 228; Freedman, *Origins of Peasant Servitude*, 81–82.
166. Bonnassie, *La Catalogne*, 2: 773.

them. Though the relationship of lord and vassal was one of publicly declared friendship, the code recognized how such promises might end. While providing a peaceful means for severing feudal ties with their formal negation, this formula, the *diffidamentum*, was eventually viewed as an open vassalic "declaration of war" against a lord.[167] The vast majority of disputes between feudal parties centered on default of service. Interestingly, the code differentiates between premeditated dereliction and that engaged in during a fit of anger. In the first case, the offending vassal would lose his fief and could never regain it; in the second, the vassal might regain his master's love by taking another oath of homage and posting a surety with his lord to guarantee future compliance with the terms of the pact.[168] When disputes erupted into open war, the *Usatges* rules on treason came into play. The most serious forms of "treason" (*maxima bausia*) were the vassalic murder of a lord or his son, adultery with the lord's wife, or usurpation of a lord's castle. Lesser treason was caused by the vassal's refusal to carry out his conventional duties. The first form of treason could not be emended by the vassal; the second was rectified by his posting of a surety and acceptance of lordly terms of reimbursement, no matter how galling. If the traitor or *bauzator* refused to accept these peace terms, he might claim judgment from the count of Barcelona's court, where the offender could clear himself by oath or judicial battle.[169]

The place of the count of Barcelona in this mesh of feudal ties was expressed in terms of feudal reality and princely aspiration. As one of the greatest feudal luminaries of the land, the count had all the rights and responsibilities of any other lord. As the result of his office and the prestige that accrued to it from Ramón Berenguer I's victories over his rebellious nobility, the count possessed at least a symbolic superiority over the other Catalan counts and magnates. His court, constituted much like those of other lords, was the most important since it could at times include all the great lords of Catalonia, was the source of many "new knights" (*novellos milites*), and functioned as a last court of appeals for the settlement of feudal disputes.[170] If a vassal was accused of treason but refused to have his "crimes" judged by his own lord, the case could be aired "before the prince

167. Rodón Binué, *El lenguaje técnico*, xviii, 12–14; Francesch Carreras i Candi and Siegfried Bosch, "Desafiaments de Catalunya en segle XVI," *BRABLB* 16(1933–36): 134–36.

168. *Usatges*, arts. 34–35, 99, pp. 78, 134.

169. *Usatges*, arts. 25–26, 37–38, 40, 42, pp. 72, 80, 82, 84.

170. *CDACA* 4: doc. 23, pp. 55–57; *CAVC* 1, pt. 1: 52–54; *LFM* 2: docs. 511, 526, pp. 24–25, 40–41; Valls Taberner, "Cour comtale," 271–72.

and his court." The count's role as supreme judge also made him a legal protector not only of his own men but also of all other vassals of his lands who were "unjustly oppressed by their lords."[171]

Beyond the affirmation of the judicial prestige of his court, the count was not endowed with the powers of a full-fledged suzerainty. Instead, the creators of the *Usatges* attempted to order the nobility and feudal procedure by the authority of the count of Barcelona not as eminent lord but rather as prince. With the arrangement of emendations in article 4, one of the oldest sections of the code, a "noble hierarchy" is formally laid out from "viscount" (*vicecomes*) to "comitor" (*comitor*) to "vasvassor" (*vasvassor*) to "knight" (*miles*). At the apex of this status pyramid stood the count of Barcelona and, by implication, the other Catalan counts.[172] Rather than claiming a feudal supremacy over his fellow counts which he could enforce only with the greatest of efforts, the Barcelona ruler and his legists opted to subordinate the entire network of feudal relations to a "regalian principate" which sought to bring all of Catalonia under its authority.[173] A broader territorial focus was asserted for the count of Barcelona's dominion, which now touched all residents of both Old and New Catalonia, no matter what their feudal connection to the count. His self-affirmed sovereignty functioned in the protection of all his subjects and in his even-handed rendering of justice to them, no matter what their status. Princely power was also defined in a restrictive way, with the formulation of a public prerogative which claimed for itself and itself alone, the control of defensible sites, the building of castles, the possession or use of war machines or any advanced military technology, the declaration of war and peace with Spanish Islam, and the judgment or punishment of any criminal act. The well-being of the ruler also far outweighed that of any feudal lord. If he was threatened with danger, all men, "knights and footmen alike," had to come to the aid of the sovereign under pain of being charged with dereliction of duty.[174] As Thomas Bisson has observed, the *Usatges* are a "regalian code" which regulates feudal relations, property, rank, and national security."[175] The code, however, did not always function in this way. In the long series of Catalan baronial rebellions of the thirteenth century, rebel and sovereign

---

171. *Usatges*, arts. 40, 42, 67, pp. 82–84, 104.

172. *Usatges*, art. 4, p. 54; Bonnassie, *La Catalogne*, 2: 783; Bonnassie, *Slavery*, 196–97; Bisson, "Feudalism," 184–85.

173. Bisson, "Feudalism," 185.

174. *Usatges*, arts. 64, 68, 73, pp. 102, 106, 112; Bisson, "Problem," 467.

175. Bisson, "Problem," 467.

both claimed the *Usatges* as the legal basis for litigation, breaking off relations, or even war.[176] In spite of the intentions of its creators, the code would come to be a very different law to different people.

From Court Usage to Fundamental Law

The track of custom has no one author but rather came about "because many generations were passing that way."[177] The path which took the "court usages" of the Count of Barcelona to the status as fundamental Catalan law was also unplanned and yet widened into a virtual thoroughfare as more and more segments of Catalan society claimed the code as their own. Even after Catalonia had changed to such an extent that the *Usatges* were not readily applicable, the code still enjoyed "an indubitable observance" among the Catalans. As the autonomy of the Catalan people began to wane in the early modern period, it turned to its old laws as a validating mark of a distinct nationality. This guaranteed the significance of the Usatges from century to century as much in cultural as in legal terms.

A twelfth-century law code could hardly have attained a position of such prominence without the active sponsorship of the count of Barcelona. As his military prowess brought widening bands of territory under his jurisdiction, the count was careful to prescribe either full or partial use of the code in his new domains. The same judicial expansion was discernible in the Pyrenean counties that slowly came under the count's political aegis through the twelfth and thirteenth centuries. In both forms of comital expansion, the *Usatges* were normally made an addition to local law without the removal of the latter code's status as territorial law. Thus, at Lerida in 1149, Agramunt in 1163, Tortosa in 1229, and Majorca in 1231, any number of legal procedures outlined in the *Usatges* ranging from the punishment of assault to the posting of sureties were incorporated into the local administration of justice. In the Pyrenean counties of Roussillon, Cerdanya, and Conflent, the *Usatges* were introduced between the mid-twelfth and the early fourteenth centuries.[178] Such influence for the *Usatges* was officially

176. Donald J. Kagay, "Structures of Baronial Dissent and Revolt Under James I (1213–76)," *Mediaevistik* 1 (1988): 66.

177. Nicolas S. Otto, *Derecho foral* (Barcelona: Bosch, 1954), 28–29.

178. Broca y Montagut, *Historia*, 1: 343; José Maria Font Rius, "El desarollo general del derecho en los territorios de la corona de Aragón," *VII CHCA*, 1: 304, 321; Jesús Maria Lalinde Abadía, *Iniciación histórica al derecho español* (Barcelona: Ayuntamiento de Barcelona, 1970), 160; Jean-Auguste Brutails, *Études sur la condition des populations rurales du Roussillon au*

rendered impossible in Valencia, the last of the great Muslim domains conquered by the house of Barcelona, by Jaime I's promulgation of a comprehensive law code, the *Furs*, for the kingdom in 1238. In spite of this, the northern half of the kingdom closest to Catalonia and filled with Catalan settlers informally claimed the *Usatges* as its law of choice.[179] By and large, then, the set of statutes that emerged from the Barcelona court had now spread in influence and acceptance over a remarkably large and varied territory bordered by the upland valleys of the Pyrenees over into Provence down into the Valencian *huerta* and out to the Balearic chain.

Because of this support by the count of Barcelona, the *Usatges* were to emerge as a virtual fundamental law from the beginning of the thirteenth century. Catalans of all classes claimed the law as their own and would allow no tampering with it — even by the count of Barcelona. With the increasing importance of Roman law in the thirteenth century and the general perception among the Catalan people that such imperial codes were being utilized to advance the power of the Barcelona ruler past acceptable customary limits, the *Usatges* became the vortex of baronial storms which battered the entire realm of Jaime I. Time and again, the sovereign had to endure the vilification and rebellion of his great men; an enduring grievance of the disgruntled barony was the erosion of the "written usage" by the sovereign's preference for Roman law and those trained in it. Eventually, the king could not ignore the mounting pressure against Roman law and had at least to seem to give in to it. In 1243 he decreed that only those advocates using the *Usatges* and other Catalan legal customs would be admitted to his courts. In 1251 and 1276 he patently outlawed the use of the Roman or Visigothic law in his tribunals and the practice of Roman law by any Catalan advocate. He firmly ruled that all adjudication in his land of Catalonia would be based on the *Usatges* and all subsequent comital decrees — "the approved legislation of the land."[180]

Though Jaime I was accused of undermining the written customary law his predecessors had largely nurtured into existence, his reign was crucial for the *Usatges* since he provided an intellectual environment conducive to legal scholarship in all his realms. Valencia received the *Furs*; Aragón

---

moyen âge (Paris: Imprimérie Nationale, 1891; Geneva: Slatkine-Megariotis, 1975), xxxviii–xli.

179. Roque Chabás y Lloréns, *Génesis del derecho foral de Valencia* (Valencia: Imprenta Francisco Vives Mora, 1902; reprint, 1909), 17.

180. *CAVC* I, pt. 1: arts. 1–3, pp. 137–38; Broca y Montagut, *História*, 343; Hinojosa y Naveros, "La admisión," 298.

the *Fueros de Aragón*; and Catalonia the *Commerationes* — all between 1238 and the Conqueror's death in 1276. The author of the last treatise was Pere Albert, a cathedral canon of Barcelona who served as royal judge into the 1260s. The subtitle of his work, *Custom of Catalonia Between Lords and Vassal*,[181] defined its purpose as an even fuller explanation of the feudal relationship than that afforded by the *Usatges*. The learned canon treated all the issues raised in the *Usatges* but in much more detail. Some of the matters he focused on were the nature of the act of homage, the various implications of liege lordship and vassalage, the rights and duties involved in the investiture of a fief, the powers and obligations of castellans, and the position of lord and vassal before the law. Surely, the most interesting question he posed was the relationship of the sovereignty of the Barcelona ruler to the feudal bond. Commenting on article 64, *Princeps namque*, Pere Albert plainly affirmed the superiority of the count of Barcelona's sovereignty over any feudal claim a lord might have over his own men. Vassals did not have to honor a seigneurial command to wage war against the prince since this would involve *lèse majesté* and this far outweighed vassalian dereliction of duty. The maxim Pere Albert employs in this case is significant in gauging the advancement of the political position of the count of Barcelona since first delineated in the *Usatges*: "public utility must be preferred to that of the private sector."[182] In addition to the work of Pere Albert, the *Usatges* also gave rise to another set of feudal norms, the *Customs de Catalunya*, attributed variously to the great canon himself and fourteenth-century commentator Guillem de Vallseca. These laws lack the polish of the *Commemorationes* and seem to have been fashioned for courtroom use. The very format of the work is declaratory rather than investigative; in that, a schedule of precedents concerning all phases of the feudal relationship were clarified in "simple, pragmatic fashion."[183]

Besides its influence on legists, the *Usatges*, as the oldest statement of customary law associated with the count of Barcelona, acted as a legal rudder which steered all subsequent comital legislation along a traditional

---

181. Broca y Montagut, "Juristes," 437.

182. *Joannes de Socarrats jurisconsul catalani in tractatum Petrii Alberti, canonici barchinonensis de consuetudines cataloniae inter dominos & vassalos ac nonnullis alliis que commemorationes Petri Alberti apellantur* (Barcelona: apud Johannem Gardiolam, 1551; Lyon: apud Antonium Vincentium, 1551), 417–18; *Los Usatges de Barcelona y els commemoracions de Pere Albert* ed. Josep Rovira i Ermengol (Barcelona: Editorial Barcino, 1933), 184–86; Maravall, *Estudios*, 1: 150–2.

183. Ferran Valls Taberner, "Un articulat inédit de consuetuds de Barcelona," *Obras*, 2: 142–47.

course. From the reign of Jaime I, the sovereign was formally bound to respect the expanding corpus of Catalan law that came to be known as the *Constitucions de Catalunya*. This body of law, which included the *Usatges*, the *Commemorationes*, all parliamentary statutes, and major comital decrees, was seen by Catalans as a legal birthright which each new count of Barcelona from Pedro II onward had to swear to uphold before he was crowned.[184] Protection of rights and prerogatives often pitted count against people in the last century and a half of the Barcelona dynasty's existence. Each side found sustenance to carry out their fight in the *Constitucions*, most especially in the *Usatges*. The sovereign could rely on the principal articles to advance his authority while the people could measure the actions of the ruler against the national law to determine if they were arbitrary and should be resisted.[185] In some cases, the same articles were employed in very different ways within the various strata of Catalan society. The most pressing points of contention centered on the control of fiefs and the level of service they enforced on the tenant. The ruler insisted that all his people, both vassals and non-vassals alike, had to aid him militarily whenever he required it. The nobles, on the other hand, quoted their traditional laws to put limits on such service.[186] The usual arena for the citing and reciting of an often-anachronistic law in support of present policies was the parliament. In opening addresses to the Catalan parliament (*Corts*), rulers from Jaime I to Martin I were always careful to emphasize that the measures laid before the assembly were "constitutional," that is, in line with the fundamental law. Members of each estate used their assent to the present business laid before them by the Crown to air past "grievances" (*greujes*); such complaints had an evident connection to legal principles laid out in the *Usatges*.[187]

Even after the *Constitucions* attained the status of fundamental law, detailed knowledge of such a massive, ever-expanding legal edifice proved a formidable task. From the reign of Jaime II (1291–1327), the Crown attempted to disseminate such knowledge on several fronts. In 1300, the sovereign established a plan to see that Catalan law was kept up-to-date,

---

184. Lalinde Abadía, *Iniciación* 160–61; Maravall, *Estudios*, 1: 148–49; Alfonso Garcia Gallo, *Curso de historia del derecho español*, 2 vols. (Madrid: 1947), 1: 266–67.

185. Kagay, "Structures," 66.

186. ACA, Cancillería real, R. 9, f. 67, R. 12, f. 113; ACA, Pergaminos de Jaime I, nos. 1257, 2146, 2186.

187. *CAVC* I, pt. 2: 404, 420–21; 3: 28; *Parlaments a les corts catalanes*, ed. Ricard Albert and Joan Gassitot, *Els Nostres Classics*, 19–20 (Barcelona: Editorial Barcino, 1928), 123.

widely known, and observed. He promised he would consult legal experts if laws needed modernizing and then lay the changes before the parliament for its approval. To assure all the laws were obeyed, a board composed of a knight, a townsman, and a lawyer would be designated in the jurisdiction of each royal vicar to monitor infractions of the law and inform the proper official.[188] Jaime II's efforts at extending the influence of Catalan law were extended in 1321 when he appointed an investigative panel of prelates, barons, knights, and townsmen to aid in making the laws more relevant to the rapidly changing, Catalan society.[189] This attempt at legal streamlining was slow to bear fruit, and in 1406 Jaime II's grandson Martin I (1395–1410) renewed royal efforts to make the law of the Catalan land more useable by reconstituting the board of 1321 and its mandate.[190] When a new sovereign, a Castilian prince of the Trastámara line, Ferran de Antequera, was installed in 1412, the Catalans, in a parliament of the next year, petitioned him to allow the translation of Catalan law from Latin to the "vulgar Catalan tongue."[191] The huge undertaking required the use of all copies of the code, treatises, and law collections maintained in comital archive in the "greater palace of Barcelona." A team of legists headed by Jaime Callis and Narcis de Sant Dionis, completed the work and presented it to Ferran's son Alfonso V the Magnanimous in 1422.[192] This process of codification did not end there, and by 1495 Catalan law was presented in another edition known as the *Constitucions y altres drets de Catalunya*. This collection, which consisted of the *Usatges*, peace and truce decrees, feudal laws such as the works of Pere Albert, parliamentary statutes, and royal decrees, was the work of Catalan legal experts who had not been commissioned by the Crown; it very quickly, however, attained an official character.[193] Subsequent editions of the compilation in 1588–9 and 1704 incorporated parliamentary laws and royal decrees issued after 1495. These later editions were official expressions of Catalan law, having been suggested and approved by the Catalan parliament.[194]

188. *BE* Ms. Z, j, 4, ff. 74r–v, 76v, 77; *CAVC* I, pt. 1: arts 1, 9, 14, 25, 28, 34, pp. 167, 172–73; Lalinde Abadía, *Iniciación*, 162.

189. BE Ms. Z, j, 4, ff. 86r–v; ACA, Cancillería real R. 220, ff. 90v, 91; CAVC I, pt. 1: arts. 9, 10, 17, 19, pp. 261, 263–64.

190. Jan Read, *The Catalans* (London: Faber and Faber, 1978), 106–8.

191. *CAVC* 11: art. 9, pp. 245, 281–83; Wolf, "Gesetzgebung," *Handbuch*, 1: 688.

192. *Constitucions de Catalunya*, ed. Josep M. Font Rius, vol. 4/1 of *Textos juridics catalans lleis i costums* (Barcelona: Generalitat de Catalunya, Departament de Justicia, 1988), xvii–xx.

193. *Constitucions*, lxv–cix; Wolf, "Gesetzgebung," *Handbuch*, 1: 689.

194. *Constitucions*, cxxvii–cxxxvii; Read, *The Catalans*, 147; Wolf, "Gesetzgebung," *Handbuch*, 1: 690.

While the cohesion of the Catalan law rested first with the approval and then the command of the ruler of Catalonia, none of the juridical collections, no matter how logically presented, gave him the full measure of sovereignty he desired. From the era of Pedro IV the Ceremonious, the Crown turned with some regularity to the Castilian legal masterwork, the *Siete Partidas*, in an attempt to delineate a royalty with much broader powers than allowed in Catalan law.[195] The populace of the region, at least that portion of it represented in the *Corts*, was not slow to recognize the implication of such actions by their ruler and repeatedly raised the alarm that the liberties defined in the *Constitucions* were at risk. The interregnum preceding the accession of the Trastámara dynasty convinced political authorities in all three realms of the Crown of Aragon that an expanded governing role for the parliament was not only possible but absolutely necessary. The second sovereign of the new dynasty, Alfonso V (1416–58), bore the brunt of the virtual parliamentary rebellion directed against a creeping Castilianization within the Catalan government. The remedies proposed to Alfonso by the Catalan *Corts* between 1419 and 1423 insisted that earlier statutes allowing only Catalans to serve as public servants in the Principate be honored fully and all royal actions that violated the body of Catalan law would be considered invalid by the Catalan public. The king avoided the nagging problem of the Catalans and spent most of his reign in making good a claim to the Kingdom of Naples, while leaving his wife Maria of Castile to administer Catalonia as lieutenant general.[196] Significantly, much of what the Catalans wanted from their new Trastámara rulers centered on a return to the traditional political compact between sovereign and people which had been worked out during the centuries of its rule by the Barcelona dynasty. The *Usatges* and *Constitucions* stood as the blueprint for this covenant of rule and thus had to be scrupulously followed by count and *Corts*. With the union of Castile and the Crown of Aragon in 1479, the Catalans would return time and again to their traditional laws to recall an era of lost glory and define their own aspirations of nationhood in the political orbit with Madrid at its center.

Catalonia's great potential for rebellion throughout the early modern era was often sparked by fervent attachment to its traditional laws. To mollify their troublesome Catalan subjects, the Catholic kings and their Hapsburg successors all came to Barcelona and, as counts of Barcelona,

195. Ramon d'Abadal i de Vinyals, "Les *partidas* y Catalunya," *EUC* 6(1912): 13–37, 161–81; Font Rius, "Desarrollo," 301.

196. Bisson, *Medieval Crown*, 41–43.

swore that all laws of the realm from the *Usatges* onward would be "inviolably observed."[197] Even when Spain fell under French dominance with the installation of the Bourbon dynasty, the first ruler of this line, Felipe V (1700–16) was quick to recognize that the Catalans were "restless and jealous of their privileges" and tried to pacify them whenever possible.[198] This mainly consisted in declaring respect for their traditional laws. It was only when international stresses came into play with the War of Spanish Succession (1700–14) that the fate of Catalonia and all manifestations of her culture were sealed. When the Catalans formally abrogated their allegiance to Felipe V in 1705, they were assured by their new Austrian, English, and Dutch allies that their "Laws and Privileges [would] be fully maintained and preserved." With a Bourbon victory in 1714, these promises proved to be worth nothing, and Catalonia went into the first of two eras of darkness which recent history has held in store for it. Furious at the Catalan rebels and anxious to install uniform laws in all of his lands, Felipe V enacted his *Decreto de Nueva Planta* or "Decree of the New Foundation" in 1716 by which the use of the Catalan language was forbidden and the "fueros, usages, and customs" of Catalonia were replaced by a standard, Spanish code.[199]

In the two centuries after the passage of this decree, the *Usatges* and all the indigenous laws of Catalonia were kept alive as cultural symbols which reminded the region of its lost autonomy. The suppressed codes, rather than disappearing from Catalan public memory, spurred intensive research and textual criticism throughout the nineteenth century. Political reformers, such as Pi y Margall and Prat de la Riba, peered below the Castilian domination imposed on the formerly autonomous regions of the Peninsula and saw that the potential for destablilization was truly explosive. To defuse this dangerous situation, both thinkers argued for a federal arrangement not unlike that of Switzerland or the United States in which each of the Peninsula's regions would retain their long-held laws but would have them upgraded in line with general Spanish law.[200] By 1871 the ideologues had

197. ACA, Colección de Códigos, no. 379/963 ff. 41v, 82v; John Lynch, *Spain Under the Hapsburgs*, 2 vols. (Oxford: Oxford University Press 1965–78; New York: New York University Press, 1981), 1: 197; Read, *The Catalans*, 117.

198. Read, *The Catalans*, 147.

199. Read, *The Catalans*, 148, 152.

200. Read, *The Catalans*, 180; Francisco Pi y Margall, *Las nacionalidades* (Madrid: Imprenta y Libreria de E. Martinez, 1877: Madrid: Centro de Estudios Constituciónales, 1986), 273.

their chance to form a new Spain, one fashioned on the "principle of unity in variety," with the proclamation of the first Republic, but this confused experiment in liberal rule was overthrown by a military coup that quickly restored the monarchy.[201] It was not until the abdication of Alfonso XIII in 1931 and the issuance of the *Catalan Statute* in September, 1932, however, that the dream of a Catalonia with control over its internal affairs could be realized. One of the first acts of the restored parliamentary ruling committee, the *Generalitat*, was the formal restoration of the region's long-suppressed corpus of law.

Yet with the final victory of Francisco Franco in 1939 all such gains were erased and a Bourbon-like repression fell over northeastern Spain once more. Long before the death of the *Caudillo* in 1971, however, Catalonia had slowly begun to recover its importance first in economic terms but finally in the spheres of politics and culture.[202] This thawing of centralist constraint would bring Catalonia's fundamental laws back into their own with the enactment of the *Compilación del Derecho Civil* in 1960. The circle from law to cultural icon and back again had thus been completed. As a bellwether of Catalan nationalism, then, the *Usatges* had presaged the course of the Catalan state from the unifying suppression by Castile to a broadbased autonomy within the Spanish state.

Trends of *Usatges* Scholarship

The unique place of *Usatges* in Catalan society is mirrored by the long history of study and controversy the laws have engendered. Because of the anomalies of the code and uncertainties concerning its authorship and date of composition, scholarship concerning the *Usatges* has led to many variant conclusions about its very development. The headwaters of all *Usatges* research is a passage in Catalonia's first great chronicle, the late twelfth-century *Gesta Comitum Barchinonensium*, which claimed that Ramón Berenguer I,

---

201. Joseph August Brandt, *Toward the New Spain: The Spanish Revolution of 1868 and the First Republic* (Chicago: University of Chicago Press, 1933; Philadelphia: Porcupine Press, 1976), 120.

202. Eduardo López-Aranguren, "Autonomía y descentralización: Las relaciónes entre el poder central y los poderes autonomicos," *Las nacionalidades del estado español: Una problematica cultural* (Minneapolis: University of Minnesota Press, 1986), 69; Read, *The Catalans*, 186, 198.

wishing to distinguish his rule, before the Cardinal and Roman Legate Ugo [Candidus] and very many magnates within the Palace of Barcelona and, with the counsel and assent of the aforesaid, decreed certain of his own laws which we call the Usatges of Barcelona.[203]

This passage seems to support article 3 of the code which asserts that it came into being at a meeting of Ramón Berenguer I, his wife, and eighteen court barons.[204] Although none of the extant records of the Count's assemblies fit the *Gesta* model, this "historical" reference, coupled with the code's prologue, has formed the basis for the work of a group of legists and historians who assumed that the *Usatges* became a written code in the mid-eleventh century. The first proponents of this view were a series of Catalan glossators and commentators including Pere Albert and Jaume de Montjuich in the thirteenth century; Guillem and Jaume de Vallseca and Jaume Callis in the fourteenth century; and Jaume de Marquilles in the fifteenth.[205] To all of these legists, the *Usatges* was not a spent force in the legal life of Catalonia but rather the fundament of the region's law. As such, the code deserved exhaustive study and research. Though they could not agree on the exact date of the work's composition, they agreed that it was in the last half of Ramón Berenguer I's reign. Dating of the code, however, was only one of their tasks for by their exhaustive commentaries, they traced the influence of the *Usatges* on the legal practices of their own day. The influence of the code in the Pyrenean counties and into Occitania was likewise explored by antiquaries such as Andreu Bosch and historians as J. Massot-Reynier and Jean-Auguste Brutails.[206]

The nineteenth century ushered in a more thorough and scientific investigation of the *Usatges*. Through the researches of such scholars as Pedro Nolasco in 1868[207] and Fidel Fita y Colomé and Bienvenido Oliver y Esteller in 1897,[208] a rectified text of the *Constitucions* was established in Latin and a Castilian translation of the same body of law also came into

203. *GCB* chap. 11, p. 32; *CSJP* chap. 29, p. 47.

204. *Usatges*, art. 3, pp. 52–54.

205. *Diccionari biogràfic*, 4 vols. (Barcelona: Albertí Editor, 1966–1970), 1: 39–41; 3: 76, 273; 4: 420.

206. Andreu Bosch, *Summari, index, o epitome dels admirales y nobilissims lo tots de honor de Catalunya, Rosello, y Cerdanya* (Perpignan, 1628), 515–16; J. Massot-Reynier, *Les coutomes de Perpignan* (Montpellier: J. Martel, aine imprimieur de la Société Archéologique, 1848; Marseilles: Laffitte Reprints, 1976), lxiv–lxvii; Brutails, *Études*, xxxvii–xl.

207. See listing in Bibliography under manuscript editions.

208. Bienvenido Oliver y Esteller, *Historia de derecho en Cataluña, Mallorca, y Valencia, y del código de los costumbres de Tortosa*, 4 vols. (Madrid: Imprenta de Miguel Ginesta, 1876), 1: 260–78.

being. In both editions, the laws were arranged according to subject. Several important monographs and articles concerning the *Usatges* appeared in the latter half of the century. Three Spanish scholars, José Botet y Sisó,[209] Fidel Fita y Colomé,[210] and José Coroleu i Pella,[211] each created a topical apparatus for the laws and then produced lengthy commentaries on various articles of the code. As far as the date of composition and authorship of the *Usatges*, they each followed the general assumption of the Catalan legists. These widely accepted points were soon challenged and from far afield. In 1886 a German legal historian, Julius Ficker, systematically demolished the idea that the code was the work of a single legislator and showed it to be the product of a number of compilers, at least one of whom was familiar with the revival of Roman jurisprudence which took place in southern France and Italy during the twelfth century. He did this by showing that many of the code's articles were borrowed from Isidore of Seville, the *Liber Judiciorum*, and the *Exceptiones Legum Romanorum* (an Occitanian legal manual of the twelfth century).[212] An element of controversy—the first of many—had been dispassionately placed in the midst of *Usatges* research but would not alter its course until eighty years and a civil war had passed.

The first years of the twentieth century saw the drive for better *Usatges* texts continuing unabated. In 1907 Arturo Corbella y Pascual[213] attempted to perfect the 1897 edition with a concordance of two fifteenth-century Latin texts, while Mossen Josep Gudiol[214] published the first edition of a thirteenth-century Catalan translation of the laws. What was long considered the definitive edition of the code appeared in 1913 when two of Catalonia's greatest historians, Ramon d'Abadal i de Vinyals and Ferran Valls Taberner, collaborated to produce a Latin and Catalan version based

209. José Botet y Sisó, "Los usatges de Barcelona: Estudis historichs y crítichs de la primer compilació de lleys catalans," *La Renexansa* 1(1871): 17–18, 29–31, 41–43, 53–57, 73–75.

210. Fidel Fita y Colomé, "Código de los Usajes de Barcelona," *BRAH* 27(1890): 389–93.

211. José Coroleu y Pella, "Código de los usajes de Barcelona. Estudio critico," *BRAH* 4(1884): 83–104.

212. Julius Ficker, "Über die *Usatici Barchinonae* und deren zu sammenhan mit den *Exceptiones Legum Romanorum*," *Mitteilungen des Instituts fur österreichische Geschictsforshung* 1(1886): 136–275; Ferran Valls Taberner, "Les descobertes de Ficker sobre els *Usatges de Barcelona* i llurs affinitats amb les '*Exceptiones Legum Romanorum*'," *Obras*, 2: 37–44.

213. Arturo Corbella y Pascual, "Concordancia entre el texto catalan oficial y los latinos de Amoros y Ferrer y ensayo de restitución del texto primitivo de la colección denominada Usajes de Barcelona," *Revista Jurídica de Catalunya* 13(1907): 156–76.

214. See listing in manuscript editions section.

on several early texts.[215] The ghost of Ficker's work had to be laid to rest, however, and thus a whole array of scholars set out to explain the anomalies of the code. Their principal task was the admission that the *Usatges* was not a monolithic work and came into existence over some years. The great Catalan antiquarian, José Balari Jovany, concluded that this era had to be the years of Ramon Berenguer I's ascendancy (1053–71).[216] The Spanish legal historian Guillermo Maria de Broca y Montagut, following Ficker, disagreed and claimed that the code was in the making from the mid-eleventh to the thirteenth century.[217] The conundrum of the code's origin was seemingly unraveled by one of its many editors, Valls Taberner. Agreeing with Ficker that the laws were not the work of a single legislative session, he violently disagreed with the German scholar's contention and that of his colleague d'Abadal i de Vinyals that the redaction of some sections of the code took place in the twelfth century or even later. He set out his views in a series of articles which appeared in Spanish and Catalan scholarly journals before the Spanish Civil War. In these studies, he proposed that the *Usatges* were promulgated in four stages between 1058 and 1068 as the result of small assemblies summoned by Ramon Berenguer I. These laws were then edited into a unified entity at some time before the count's death in 1076.[218] Valls Taberner had apparently solved the *Usatges* puzzle and his views became a point of Catalan academic orthodoxy on the subject for the next quarter century. His work provided the chronological framework for the popular celebration of the code's existence which began in 1958. The date was heralded by the popular articles of Antoni Borell Macia[219] and José Maria Font Rius[220] which disseminated the accepted views on the code to the general Catalan reading public and readied it for the promulgation of a new set of laws for Catalonia which were drawn from her medieval past. Ironically, it was during the conferences which accompanied the enactment of the *Compilación* in July of 1960 that the fissures in the traditional view of the formation of the *Usatges* outlined in the Valls Taberner thesis became increasingly evident.

215. See listing in manuscript editions section.

216. Balari, *Origenes históricos*, 2: 451–68.

217. Broca y Montagut, *Història*, 1: 141–79.

218. Ferran Valls Taberner, "El cardenal Hug Candid i els *Usatges de Barcelona*–l'estatut comtal de 1064," *Obras*, 2: 76–88; Valls Taberner, "Usatges del Comte Ramon Berenguer III del Barcelona," *Obras*, 2: 89–93; Valls Taberner, "Noves recerques sobre els *Usatges de Barcelona*," *EUC* 20(1936): 70–83.

219. Antoni Borrell Macia, "Els *Usatges*: Primer codi de costums d'occident," *Cristianidad* 338(April 1–15, 1958): 226.

220. José Maria Font Rius, "En IX centenario del primer código catalan: Los *Usatges de Barcelona*," *Cristianidad* 338(April 1–15, 1959): 220–22.

The fragmentation of the historical theory which had all but attained the status of dogma really began in 1913 when Ramón d'Abadal i Vinyals asserted that no exact dating could be posited for the code because it was composed of different sources from different eras.[221] In the wake of the Catalan glorification of its first law code in 1958, the Italian scholar Guido Carlo Mor made a close comparison of the earliest Latin and Catalan texts of the laws in order to determine which parts of the code belonged to the original written version and which were glosses or interpolations. From this analysis, he concluded that some of the *Usatges* articles were indeed of an eleventh-century vintage but that the first finished form of the laws appeared in the mid-twelfth century.[222] Mor's resuscitation of a venue of research originating with Julius Ficker gave rise to what Thomas Bisson has characterized as "one of the most important revisions in medieval Hispanic studies."[223] Though Mor's theory was widely ignored or violently opposed, it was accepted by one very influential adherent in the decade after its appearance; for, from 1963, the dean of Catalan historians, Ramón d'Abadal i de Vinyals, reiterated his belief that the *Usatges* were heterogenous in structure or authorship. In 1966 he publicly broke with the view of his colleague Valls Taberner on the subject by writing:

> It is necessary to surrender oneself to the acceptance that the compilation of the *Usatges* is not the work of Ramón Berenguer I nor of his immediate successors but the creation of the Romanizing legists of the court of Ramón Berenguer IV.[224]

Though d'Abadal i de Vinyals died shortly after this statement was made, the weight of his reputation guaranteed that the views of Valls Taberner would no longer monopolize *Usatges* research. Within a decade, new studies expanding on d'Abadal i de Vinyals' premise had begun to appear. In 1975–76 the French historian Pierre Bonnassie turned his attention to the "problem of the *Usatges of Barcelona*" in the course of his monumental two-volume study of early medieval Catalonia. He attempted to determine whether a small core of the code may indeed have been issued during the reign of Ramón Berenguer I but the principal evidence he used to bolster this contention was the citation of five of the code's articles in which eleventh-century coinage systems are mentioned. More significant

221. *Usatges*, ed. d'Abadal and Valls Taberner, xi.
222. Mor, "En torno," 412–59.
223. Bisson, "Problem," 466.
224. d'Abadal i de Vinyals, "La vida politica," 14: xlviii–xlix; Bonnassie, *La Catalogne*, 2: 713, n. 83.

for the traditional argument concerning the code's origins was his examination of Catalan juridical records between 1060 and 1075. These clearly showed that "a legal usage of Barcelona" (*usum de Barchinona*) had really begun to evolve during the reign of Ramón Berenguer "the Old."[225]

Following closely on Bonnassie's researches came what must be considered the most cogent explanation to date of the *Usatges'* formation. It was presented in 1977 at a Catalan academic conclave by the Catalan philologist Joan Bastardas i Parera.[226] Resolving to strip away the textual detritus of the code's many editions and get at its core, Bastardas i Parera, like Mor, isolated its earliest Latin and Catalan editions — all from the mid-thirteenth century. By a "rigorous criticism" of these texts, he was able to determine which of the articles were original and which had been appended to the text in the process of copying and recopying. Delineating the relationship between the parts of the code, Bastardas i Parera then set its emergence within a definite time framework by reviewing twelfth-century references to Catalonia's customary law to discover when this *consuetudo Barchinone* actually referred to the *Usatges*. By reinterpreting evidence that had long been available to investigators of the code, in one stroke he seemed to resolve the "enigma of the *Usatges*" and in 1984 published his rectified Catalan and Latin edition of the laws which has formed the basis of this English translation.[227]

One of the other participants of the 1977 conference, José Maria Font Rius, portrayed Bastardas i Parera's work as a "brilliant manifestation of the possibilities philology may offer to the study of a medieval juridical text."[228] He was also quick to add that this new solution should not hamper but rather spur further research on the code. This call was quickly heeded in 1977 as Aquilino Iglesia Ferreirós published the first installment of his essay on the history of Catalan law. He traced the "death-agony" of Visigothic law from the eighth to the eleventh century and its gradual replacement by Catalan customary law. As far as the composition and dating of the *Usatges* go, Iglesia Ferreirós accepted the Bastardas i Parera thesis in its entirety.[229] The same can be said of the American scholar Bisson who in two seminal articles of 1978 and 1980 dealt with the *Usatges* in the context of studies on the emerging political and social systems in the Crown of Aragon in the

---

225. Bonnassie, *La Catalogne*, 2: 711–28.
226. Joan Bastardas i Parera, *La problematica de Usatges*, 1–31.
227. See listing under manuscript editions section.
228. Font Rius, *Compilación*, 58.
229. Iglesia Ferreirós, "La creación de derecho," 253–83.

twelfth and thirteenth centuries. Authorship and dating of the code were not Bisson's prime concern, since these questions seemed suitably answered by Bastardas i Parera.[230] Instead, he focused on the place of the *Usatges* in regard to Catalan law, kingship, and feudalism.

The Bastardas i Parera thesis has proved the dominant theory of *Usatges* research in the past decade. However, it has not won over all elements of the Spanish academic world, as is evidenced by a reissue in 1984 of Valls Taberner's articles on the code as well as the 1913 edition of the code.[231] A year later, the entire issue of Catalan feudalism was addressed in an important conference at the University of Gerona. The published edition of the proceedings, entitled *La formació i expansió del feudalisme català*, appeared in 1986. It included discussions of various aspects of Catalan feudalism and its influence on such neighboring regions as Majorca, Valencia, Castile, and Provence. The most significant of these articles in regard to *Usatges* scholarship is that of Frederic Udina Martorell and his son Antoni Maria Udina i Abelló. Reviewing the work of earlier scholars from Julius Ficker onward concerning the nature of the *Usatges*, the two authors concluded from several lines of eleventh-century evidence that over twenty of the articles included in the first redaction of the code had indeed been issued during the reign of Ramón Berenguer I. Besides their theory about the extent and nature of the *Usatici Barchinonae*, the Udinas provide an invaluable chart which details the research of Ficker, Broca, Valls Taberner, d'Abadal, Mor, Bonnassie, and Bastardas i Parera concerning the "court usages."[232] While helpful to the student of the *Usatges*, this appendix also graphically displays the difficulties associated with understanding the origins of the code and shows how many different solutions this same mystery has spawned in the last century.

Conclusion

The law code known as the *Usatges of Barcelona* holds a paramount place in the legal development of Catalonia; its cultural significance for the region cannot be overstated. It epitomizes a heritage which is distinctly Catalan. This position of preeminence for a medieval collection of laws may have

---

230. Bisson, "Problem," 466–69; Bisson, "Feudalism," 184–85.
231. Fernando Valls Taberner, *Los Usatges de Barcelona: Estudios, comentarios y edición bilingüe del texto*, ed. Manuel J. Pelaez and Enrique M. Guerra (Malaga/Barcelona: Universidad de Malaga/Promociónes Publicaciónes Universitarias, 1984).
232. Udina Martorell and Udina i Abelló, "Consideracións," 102–4.

faded as Catalonia advanced into the industrial era but for the centralizing efforts of a Madrid government which the Catalans looked on as an agency of foreign oppression. Their law, language, and all other marks of cultural individuality were long suppressed by the national government, and yet they did not die. The career of the *Usatges* in the contemporary world should be taken as an example of a fundamental political paradigm for the aging modern world in which we live. As evident from recent events in Eastern Europe and the Middle and Far East, suppression of the legal and cultural norms of once-independent domains by a national government acting in the name of centralization does not eradicate these forms but may instead make of them cultural exemplars, which are revered by generation after generation until called on as a rallying cry for independence or at least greater autonomy within the framework of the nation state. With these considerations in mind, the *Usatges of Barcelona* still has and presumably always will have a place in the Catalan world.

Manuscripts and Editions

Texts of the *Usatges of Barcelona* have survived in both Latin and Catalan versions in a number of European libraries. Understandably, the majority of these are in the Iberian Peninsula. The most important of these copies, published between the thirteenth and fifteenth century, are:

(1) Ms. Z,78 i, 3; Z, ii, 4; Z, ii, 16; and Ms. Z, iii, 14 of the Real biblioteca de San Lorenzo de Escorial
(2) Ms. 9-9-7/2005 of the Academía de la história, Madrid.
(3) Ms. Vitr. II, 20.A2119 of the Col.legi d'advocats de Barcelona.
(4) Ms. 12.691 of the Biblioteca nacional, Madrid.
(5) Cancillería real, Papeles a incorporar, Legislación, caja 1, num. 1 of Archivo de la corona de Aragón.

The most important manuscripts of the *Usatges* in foreign libraries are:

(1) Mss. 4673 and 4792 of the Bibliothèque Nationale de Paris
(2) Ms. 3058 of the Collectio ottobonica, Vatican Library.

Printed editions of the Usatges have appeared in large collections of

Catalan law and in specific redactions,commentaries, and translations. The most important of the first category are

(1) *Constitucions de Cataluña y altres drets de Catalunya.* Barcelona: Pere Michel and Diego Gumiel, 1495.

(2) *Constitutiones y Altres Drets de Catalunya Compilats en Virtut de Capitol de Cort LXXXII de las Corts del Rey Don Philip IV Nostre Senyor Celebradas en la Ciutat de Barcelona Any MDCCII.* Barcelona: Joan Pau Marti y Joseph Llopis, Estampers, 1704. Reprint. Barcelona: Editorial Base, 1973.

In the second category, the most important works are

(1) *Antiquores barchinonensium leges, quos vulgas usaticos apellat cum comentariis supremorum jurisconsultorum Jacobi a monte Judaica, Jacobi et Guillermi Vallesicca et Jacobi Calicii.* Barcelona: NP, 1594.

(2) Pedro Nolasco Vives y Cebria, *Traducción al castellano de los usajes y demas derechos de Cataluna,* 4 vols. Barcelona: Libreria Ne Plus Ultra, 1861; Madrid: Libreria Emilio Font, 1861; Barcelona: Generalitat de Barcelona, Departament de Justicia, 1988.

(3) Fidel Fita y Colomé and Bienvenido Oliver y Esteller eds. *Usatges de Barcelona.* In *CAVC,* I, pt. 1: 3–46.

(4) Mossen Josep Gudiol, "Traducció del Usatges, les mes antiques constitucions de Catalunya y costumes de Pere Albert." *Anuari,* I(1907): 285–334.

(5) Ramon d'Abadal i de Vinyals and Ferran Valls Taberner eds. *Usatges de Barcelona, Texts de dret català,* 1. Barcelona: Diputació Provincial, 1913.

(6) Josep Rovira i Ermengol ed. *Los Usatges de Barcelona y els Commemoracions de Pere Albert.* Barcelona: Editorial Barcino, 1933.

(7) Joan Bastardas i Parera ed. *Usatges de Barcelona. El codi a mitjan segle XII.* Barcelona: Fundació Noguera, 1984.

Usage

Though the trend of American scholars of eastern Spain has been to convert all personal and place names into Catalan, I feel that this removes them from their American audience, who are much more familiar with English or Spanish forms. In regard to the sovereigns under consideration in this study, I have used the Aragonese names and regnal numbers rather than including the Catalan numeration since the former method is better known. I have followed the place name usages of Joseph O'Callaghan's *History of Medieval Spain* except in the appendix notes, where I have used the Catalan form of the region's modern provinces and lesser-known towns and villages.

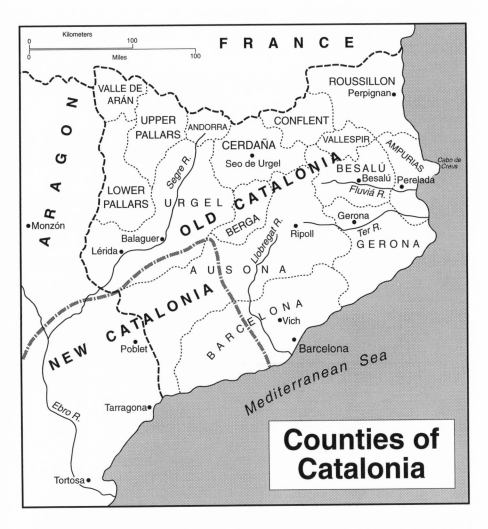

Map 1. The Counties of Catalonia

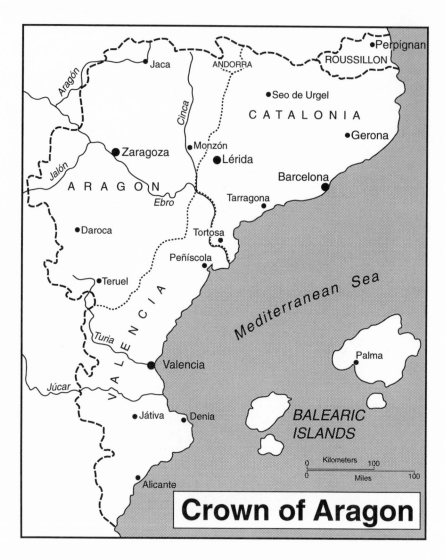

Map 2. The Crown of Aragon

The *Usatges of Barcelona*

I

Before the rules of customary law were decreed, judges customarily ruled that all offenses, if they could not be overlooked, had to be settled for all time by oath, judicial battle, or ordeal of boiling or freezing water with the utterance of the following words: "I swear to you by God and these Holy Gospels that these offenses which I have committed against you, I thus did within my rights and by your negligence." And then he would undergo the judicial battle or one of the aforesaid judgments; namely, that of freezing or boiling water.

Homicide or adultery[1] which could not be overlooked was judged, settled, or punished according to the laws and customs.[2]

2

When Lord Ramón Berenguer the Old[3] Count and Marquis of Barcelona and the subjugator of Spain[4] held dominion,[5] he saw and acknowledged that the Gothic laws could not be observed in all the claims and lawsuits of this land. He also saw that these laws did not specifically adjudicate many disputes and offenses. With the approval and counsel of his good men, along with his very prudent and wise wife Almodis, he issued and decreed the rules of customary law by which all disputes and offenses[6]

---

1. *Cugucia* denotes adultery committed by the wife. The betrayed husband was known as a *cuguç* "cuckold."
2. Whenever *lex* or law is used in the code, it refers to the great Visigothic code, the *Liber Judiciorum. Mos* or custom connotes the legal usages that had developed in the Spanish March since the eighth century.
3. The first reference to Ramón Berenguer I as "the Old" dates from 1092 during the reign of his son Berenguer Ramón II.
4. *Ispanie* "Spain" was a term used by the Christian realms of the Peninsula to describe all the Spanish territories still held by the Muslims.
5. *Honor* refers both to a fief and to the entire complex of rights and jurisdiction which a lord held in regard to his vassals.
6. *Malefactum* "offense" was both an armed attack on another and the personal harm or damage such an action might cause.

inserted therein were to be submitted to judgment, pleaded, judged, decreed, compensated, and punished. Indeed, the Count did this on the authority of the *Book of Judges*, which says: "Surely royal judgment will have the prerogative to add laws if truly new situations in suits demand it."[7] "so it may be disposed of at the discretion of royal power that once a suit is decided it should be inserted in the laws,"[8] and "indeed only the royal power will be free in everything to enforce in suits whatever penalty it deems fit."[9]

> And the rules of customary law
> which he issued so begin.

3
    These are the customary legal rules of court usages which Lord Ramon the Old, Count of Barcelona, and his wife Almodis decreed binding on their land forever with the assent and acclamation of the magnates of their land, namely,

Ponç, Viscount of Gerona

Ramón, Viscount of Cardona

Ulait, Viscount of Barcelona, as well as

Gombau de Besora

Mir Gilabert

Alaman de Cerveló

Bernat Amat de Claramunt

Ramon de Montcada

Amat Eneas

Guillem Bernat de Queralt

Arnau Mir de Sent Martí

Guillem Senescalch

Jofre Bastó

Renalt Guillem

7. This is a citation of a passage of the *Liber Judiciorum* (I, 1, 14) with the rubric: "That once lawsuits have been resolved, let them at no time be revived but let them be disposed of according to the arrangement of this book: the addition of other laws remaining one of the prerogatives of kings."
    8. A quote from the same Visigothic code (II, 1, 13) with the rubric "That no plea, which is not contained in the laws, should be heard."
    9. Another quote from the Visigothic laws (II, 5, 8) with the rubric "That no one should be bound in person or property under the terms of a contract in which deception has been used. Also concerning the penalty which may be assessed in tribunals."

Gicbert Guitart
Umbert de les Agudes
Guillem March
Bonfil March
Guillem Borrell, judges

4

Thus whoever kills, wounds, or dishonors a viscount in any way, let him make compensation to him as for two *comitores*[10]. If a *comitor*, as for two *vasvassores*.[11]

Concerning a *vasvassor* who has five knights, let a compensation of sixty ounces of seared gold[12] and thirty lashes be made for his death. And if he has more knights, let the compensation increase according to the number of knights.

Indeed let whoever kills a knight give twelve ounces of seared gold in compensation. Indeed, let whoever wounds one make a compensation to him of six ounces for one blow or many.

5

If anyone sets an ambush,[13] premeditatedly assaults a knight, beats him with a club, and pulls his hair, let him make compensation to him as for his death since this a serious dishonor. If, on the other hand, anyone in anger strikes a knight with any blow whatsoever with fist or stone, rock or club, but without drawing blood,[14] let three ounces be given him. But if there is bloodshed from the body, let four ounces be given him; from the head, five; and from the face, six.

But if one strikes a knight in his limbs so he appears incapacitated, let

---

10. A *comitor* in Latin or *comdor* in Catalan was a member of a line of middle-ranking Catalan nobility which apparently had its origins in the service of counts who held power throughout the Spanish March.

11. A *vasvassor* or *vasvasour* was a middle-grade noble who served as a "vassal of other vassals." In Catalonia, a *vasvassor* normally connoted a castellan.

12. The *uncia auri cocti* (*onçes d'aur cuyt*, Catalan) was a Muslim coin of the late tenth century which was minted in Cordova but circulated in all the Christian realms of the Peninsula.

13. *Aguait* was defined by one *Usatges* commentator Jaume Marquilles as "an evil done by aggression or assault to those traveling by." Like the Old French *imboscare*, which is the root of the English word "ambush," the "great dishonor" caused by such an action resided in the fact that the victim was attacked without formal challenge.

14. The distinction between blows causing blood flow and those which failed to and their compensation was well-established in the Visigothic code (VI, 4, 3) and in the Bavarian laws (*Laws of the Alamans and Bavarians*, trans. Rivers, IV: 1–2, p. 130).

him be compensated as for his death. Indeed if he is taken prisoner and put in shackles or leg irons[15], let him be compensated for half of the value of his death.[16] If he is attacked, beaten, wounded, put in an underground cell, or held for ransom, let the compensation be made as for his death.

If he was only taken prisoner and held under guard, suffered no insult or disgrace, and was not confined for a long time, let compensation be made through a penalty of submission[17] and homage or by his [the captive's] retaliation if he appears to be of equal rank. If the captor is of higher rank than the captive, let him provide him a knight of equal rank who shall carry out the penalty of submission and homage or undergo the captive's retaliation.

Moreover, for a knight who has two knights as his vassals settled on his fiefs and maintains one of them in his household, let all this abovesaid compensation be made to him or, in place of him, let it be made twice over.

6

Let ambush and armed pursuit[18] of a mounted horseman or attack of a castle be compensated by homage and the penalty of submission as it seems right to he who judges this case.

Let the son of a knight up to the age thirty be compensated as his father is. After this, let him be compensated as a peasant if he has not been made a knight.

7

Indeed, if a knight abandons knighthood while able to observe it, let him not in any way be judged or compensated as a knight. It is sufficient for one to lose knighthood if he does not have a horse and weapons, does not hold a knight's fee, and does not takes part in hosts and cavalcades[19] or come to tribunals and courts as a knight unless old age prevents him.

15. *Eschaza* were leg irons used for fettering or torturing prisoners.
16. In the first articles of the code (4–6), emendations were based on a person's status and the severity of the harm done him. As such, they are very reminiscent of the Visigothic laws and the other *leges barbarorum*. According to these compensations, the emendation of *mediam mortem* would equal half of the value owed for a knight's death, that is, six ounces of seared gold.
17. *Aliscara* (var. *hermiscara*) was a punishment suffered by a rebellious vassal to his offended lord. To restore normal feudal ties, the vassal had to humble himself formally before his lord, pay a security that he would keep his promises, and then restore fealty and homage.
18. *Encalz* (related to *incalciare*) could mean taking vengeance on an enemy by personal attack or through a lawsuit.
19. Differing from the *hostis* "host" or temporary army of his vassals which a lord could call together for up to three months, the *cavalcada* "cavalcade" was a short foray across enemy lines or a ceremonial vanguard.

8

Moreover, let townsmen and burghers litigate among themselves, be judged, and compensated as knights are. Moreover, let them be compensated by the ruler as *vasvassores* are.

9

Let Jews who are beaten, wounded, captured, incapacitated, and even killed be compensated according to the ruler's will.

10

If a bailiff who is a noble, eats wheaten bread daily, and rides a horse is killed, incapacitated, beaten, or held captive, let him be compensated as a knight is. Moreover, let an ignoble bailiff have half of this compensation.

11

Let the murder of a peasant or any other man who holds no rank besides being a Christian be compensated by six ounces; his wounding, by two ounces. Let his incapacitation and beating be compensated according to the law in copper sous.[20]

12

Indeed after one has compensated another for the wrong done him when he took him prisoner, let the imprisonment be compensated in this way. If the captive was released on the day of capture or the next day, let the captor give him a suitable amount from his own property and swear an oath by a man of the captive's rank that he need not compensate him further for the insult and dishonor done him. Yet if he is held longer in leg irons or shackles, placed in an underground cell, kept fettered or under guard in any way, let him receive six sous[21] in compensation for each day and night. Let ten sous be given him for having his hands and feet bound.

13

If one strikes another in the face, let five sous be given for a slap; ten sous for a blow with a fist or stone, rock, or club; and if there is blood shed from the face, twenty sous. If one pulls another's hair with one hand, let him give him five sous; with two hands, ten sous. If he throws him to the

20. Copper coin of the *ta'ifa* of Tortosa which circulated in Catalonia through much of the eleventh century.
21. Silver coinage of Ramón Berenguer I in circulation from the mid-eleventh century.

ground, fifteen sous. If he pulls him by the beard, twenty; for the shaving of his hair, forty sous.

14

If one, in anger, strikes any type of blow to another's body, let him give a single sou for each blow which does not show [leave a bruise]. For those which do, let him give two sous apiece. And if there is bloodshed from these, five sous; for the breaking of a bone in the body, fifty sous. If in angrily assaulting and dragging down another, one makes blood flow from mouth or nostrils, let him give to him twenty sous in compensation.

15

If one shoves another with one hand, let him give one sou to him; with two hands, two sous. If he throws him to the ground, let him give three sous to him.

16

If one spits in another's face, let him make compensation of twenty sous to him or suffer his retaliation.

17

If one criminally slanders[22] another and does not want to or cannot prove this about him, either let him swear an oath to him that he uttered this slander in anger and not from the truth which he then knew or let him make as much compensation to him[the victim] as he lost by this slander as if it had been the truth if the slandered wished that the slanderer should purge himself on oath concerning it.

18

Let offenses against Saracen captives be compensated as to masters for their slaves. Therefore, let their deaths be compensated according to their value. It says this since there are many of a great ransom price while others are skilled and instructed in different types of crafts.

22. A *Usatges* commentator Jaume Callis claimed that two types of *follia* "slander" existed: (1) non-criminal (that directed against peasants or said in jest); and (2) criminal (that directed against a person of equal or greater rank). As an example of this latter type, Callis cites an undated document of Vich in which one man called another a counterfeiter "in the presence of very many persons" and was accordingly accused of criminal slander.

19

Let every woman be compensated according to the rank of her husband. If she never had or does not currently have a husband, let her be compensated according to the rank of her father or brother.

20

All men must post a surety[23] for their lords wherever their lords demand it in their land. His viscounts and *comitores* must also do so for the ruler with a hundred golden ounces of Valencia[24] for each castle with its fief. Indeed, each knight must do so with ten golden ounces of Valencia for every knight's fee[25]; for a castle with its revenues[26] and for other holdings, ten; for smaller fiefs, according to their value, and indeed for an act of homage in regard to a half a knight's fee of land, concerning that which pertains to the fealty. Moreover, a peasant must do so with five sous.

21

Let a tribunal be announced among both magnates and knights for the first time up to ten days in advance; then let it be announced eight days in advance. Indeed let a tribunal be announced among peasants on the fourth or fifth day before.

Indeed his viscounts, *comitores*, *vasvassores*, and knights must attend a plea with the Count wherever he commands them within his county. But if they cannot return home on this day, let him give them a safe conduct. This must be done in the same way between viscounts, *comitores*, *vasvassores*, and other knights so that each of these must attend a plea with his liege lord from whom he holds the largest fief within the entrance of his lord's estate if the lord agrees to this. But if he does not, let each one attend pleas with him wherever in his lands he wishes. Moreover, if he cannot return on this day, let the lord give him a safe conduct.

---

23. *Firmare directum* "posting of a surety" was carried out by a vassal to assure he would perform contracted obligations with his lord and by litigants to guarantee their acceptance of a final verdict.

24. Gold coinage of the *ta'ifa* of Valencia which circulated in Catalonia in the second half of the eleventh century.

25. A *cavalleria terre* "knight's fee" was initially a grant of land sufficient in size to support a knight and his mounts. By the last half of the eleventh century, this land grant was firmly tied to the network of feudal relations and took on the proportions of other Catalan feudal grants.

26. *Ademperamentum* refers to the profit or revenue a castellan could draw from lands attached to his castle.

22

In a suit judged between a vassal and a lord, and a judgment approved and sanctioned by both parties and well secured under the lord's authority so that it would be rendered to him, let the lord first indemnify his vassal for everything he owes him in any way whatsoever, and afterwards let him receive from his vassal everything adjudged him.

23

Before a judgment by battle may be sworn to, let it be secured through a surety of two hundred golden ounces of Valencia if it must be carried out by horsemen and by one of a hundred if by foot champions, so that the victor shall be compensated for the damage which he received in the duel both to his body, horse, or weapons, and obtain that for which the duel is fought as well as all expenses he incurs in it and the defeated shall accept this matter as settled.

24

Indeed it is not fitting concerning common pleas[27] that there be more than four judicial sessions: first, in which sureties should be suitably posted by guaranties or pledges[28] as it is necessary before the arguments of both litigants are heard; second, in which the arguments should be stated and responded to, and judgements given by judges chosen by both litigants; third, in which arguments and judgements should be reviewed by the judges and, if necessary, the judgements altered, then afterwards these should be approved, sanctioned, and well secured with the approval of the judges by pledges as they had already been; and fourth, in which the lord of the suit should actually take possession of the pledges. And while he holds them, justice should be done and judgments carried out exactly as they were adjudged and sanctioned by both litigants.

25

If magnates or knights refuse to post sureties for their lords as they must do for them and, for this reason, the lords seize control of their castles or confiscate their fiefs from them, the lords need not return to them

27. Civil suits which were not necessarily settled in the Count of Barcelona's court.
28. The two forms of sureties, the *plivium* and *pignus*, were put up either by the litigant himself or his vassals to assure he would accept the tribunal's verdict.

either castles or fiefs until they have posted the surety and made restitution for all expenses which the lord incurs in the capture and garrisoning of the castle as well as in the confiscation of the fiefs. On the other hand, if the vassals give control of these, let them not post a surety with the lords until they shall recover the castle unless the lords have a war for which they need the castle or claimed lodging in the castle.[29]

26

If one refuses to give control of his castle to his lord as he is bound to give it to him and suffers a public accusation[30] for this reason and if the lord can capture the castle, let him be permitted to hold the castle along with the fiefs which the vassal holds from the castle until the rebel shall make compensation to the lord for all expenses and losses which he has incurred in the capture of the castle and its garrisoning, and promise swearing with his own hands[31] and by a written oath that control of the castle shall no longer be refused in any way.

27

If anyone, from viscount to lower knight, dies without legal provision for his fiefs, it is permissible for his lords to bestow the fiefs on whichever of the deceased's children they wish.

28

Castellans in castles which they hold for their lords must not appoint other castellans subordinate to them without the consent of their lords. But if they do so while the lords are aware of it and do not object, these appointed castellans, who are known of and not objected to, must remain. If the lords know and object, then let those [castellans] who appointed the others there dismiss them.

29. Seigneurial rights to *statica* "castle lodging" varied widely according to individual feudal pacts, yet could normally be claimed during times of war or peace for the lord and his host or retinue.

30. The purpose of the *reptamentum* "public accusation" was to justify formally the lord's confiscation of the recalcitrant vassals's fief and guarantee the support of his other vassals in bringing this often-difficult process to fruition.

31. Oath taking *manibus suis* "with his own hands" has reference to a key element of homage and fealty, the *inmixtio manuum*, the clasping of the lord's hands over those of the vassal. As with modern oathtaking, the hands were, in effect, guarantors of the truth and, by being placed on some sacred object, such as the Gospels, affirmed the oath.

29

If one grants, mortgages, or alienates his fief[32] without the consent of his lord and if the lord knows and objects, he can confiscate the fief whenever he wishes. If he knows and does not object, he cannot confiscate the fief but can seek service for it from whichever he wishes — either from the donor or the recipient. And if the service for this fief is refused him, it is permissible for him to confiscate and hold the fief under his lordship until the refused service shall be restored twice over and securities well made to the lord so the service shall not be refused him any longer.

30

Let whoever fails to serve in the hosts and cavalcades of his lord, for whom he must perform these duties, make double restitution to his lord for all damage, expenses, and losses which he caused by his dereliction of duty. Likewise, if knights on hosts or cavalcades or in the service of their lords lose anything of theirs, let their lords compensate them in so far as the knights can verify their losses.[33]

31

Whoever sees his lord in need and fails to give him the support and service which he must render him and, because of this, pays an indemnity to him, he [the vassal] must in no way recover or retain this indemnity.

32

But if the lord wishes that his vassal increase his service to him, let him enlarge his fief. But if a vassal should have what it is customary for him to have, let him serve his lord as he agreed to serve him.

33

Whoever is a liege vassal of a lord must serve him either according to the best of his ability or according to their pact. And the lord must be bound to him against all men and none against him. Moreover, no one

32. In some aspects, this passage is similar to the policy of Frederick Barbarossa's *Constitution de jure feudorum*, which warned that "no one should be allowed to sell the entire fief or any part of it without the permission of the higher lord to whom the fief pertains." These contemporary laws differed from the *Usatges* in that vassals could alienate up to half of their fiefs without lordly consent in person. In strictly feudal terms, the *fatigatio* meant a default of vassalic obligations (*History of Feudalism*, 237–38).

33. The *averamentum* (*averament*, Catalan) was an affirmation on oath that something was true. This affirmation, which essentially pitted one man's word against another, was eventually supplemented and then supplanted by evidence, documents, and witnesses.

must make liege homage except to one lord only unless he who was his first liege lord consents.

34[34]

Whoever deserts his lord while alive in battle when he could have helped him or, with evil intent, deserts him in combat must lose everything he holds from him.

35

When one driven by anger breaks ties[35] with his lord or abandons his fief to him, let his lord confiscate all which the vassal holds for him and retain it until the vassal shall return to the terms of the homage, post a surety with him, and make compensation to him with an oath for the dishonor which he has done him. After this, let him recover the fief which he has abandoned.

36

Whoever refuses to obey his lord and deliberately breaks ties with him out of haughtiness must lose forever everything he holds from him and return it to him, even if it contains some of his own property for which he has performed no service to his lord.

37

Whoever premeditatedly kills his lord or his lord's legitimate son by hand or tongue,[36] commits adultery with his lord's wife, usurps his castle from him and only returns it to him after diminishing its value, or commits an offense against him for which he cannot make restitution or compensation — and if he is convicted of one of these acts — must come under the

---

34. Compare with a law of English-Scandinavian king Cnut I (1016–35):

> Concerning the man who deserts his lord. And the man who, through cowardice, deserts his lord or his comrades on a military expedition, either by sea or by land, shall lose all that he possesses and his own life, and the lord shall take back the property and the land which he had given him. (Richard P. Abels, *Lordship and Military Obligation in Anglo-Saxon England* [Berkeley: University of California Press, 1988], 149)

35. The *diffidamentum* and its synonym *acuyndamentum* were the opposite of the *affidamentum*, the act by which feudal bonds were forged. Though this article attempted to establish a peaceful separation between disaffected lords and vassals, the *diffidamentum* (*desafiament* in Catalan) came to connote a "virtual declaration of war" between the parties and, by the fourteenth century, the term described a challenge to a duel by any parties, even those not tied feudally.

36. *vel manu vel a lingua*, that is, by direct action or by a conspiracy.

control of his lord along with everything he holds from him so his lord may do with him as he wishes since this is the greatest treason.[37]

38

Indeed, concerning other treasons and offenses for which compensation and restitution can be made, let him post a surety with his lord in accordance with the custom of his own land and let him carry out for his lord exactly what the lord rules he should.

39

Let no vassal in any way refuse to give control of his castle or post a surety for his lord just as he is bound to give control of the castle to or post a surety for his lord since as long as he refuses, he is a traitor to his lord. And if because of this, he suffers any wrong, let no compensation be made him in any way. And if the lord suffers damage or incurs expenses, let compensation be made by his vassal.

40

If anyone is accused of treason by his lord at court in the presence of the prince, he must clear himself of this treason by the judgement or approval of the prince's court. But if he refuses to do so, then the prince must compel him to submit to judgment.

41

And likewise if a lord wishes to unjustly oppress his knight or take away his fief, the ruler then must defend and come to the aid of the knight.

42

And if one is publicly accused by the ruler, he must put himself in his custody and make restitution and compensation according to the judgment of his court for the damage, wrong, and dishonor which he has done him or clear himself of treason by oath and judicial battle with one of similar rank whose fief is of the same value, bearing the loss and gain which he must incur by this duel.

We therefore say loss and gain so he shall receive as much if he wins as he shall lose if he is defeated.

---

37. The medieval concept of treason (*bauzia*) had little in common with that of the Empire. Rather than being an infraction of the sovereign's divine *majestas*, *bauzia* violated the pact which tied lord and vassal, and as such involved the malefactors as much in perjury as in treason.

43

This must be done in the same way between magnates and their knights, except that the judicial battle may not be carried out by their own hands [in person] but only through that of a vassal chosen by each party.

44

Every offense which a vassal commits against his lord or a lord against his vassal without a lodgment of complaint[38] and rupture of ties must be emended by both parties.

45

All vassals from viscounts to the lower knights holding the ruler's fief must swear fealty to him for his fief by a written oath; namely, for those things which the ruler wishes from him.

46

Let an oath always be sworn on a consecrated altar or on the Holy Gospel. And he who swears must take every oath, except those taken in treason or sedition, "according to his knowledge" and "by God and this Holy Gospel."

47

Let all vassals, knights, and peasants alike, swear to[39] their lords just as these lords act to judge them fairly in tribunals. Yet lords should never swear to their vassals.

48

Let Jews swear to Christians but Christians never swear to them.

49

The oaths of peasants who possess a homestead and work it with a yoke of oxen[40] shall be believed up to the amount of seven silver sous.

38. A *fatigatio de directo* (*fadiga de dret*, Catalan) was a declaration by a disputant that he had been deprived of justice either because his adversary would not engage in litigation or would not accept a verdict or settlement. The phrase could also mean a reprisal by the kind of legally frustrated party described in article 79. In strictly feudal terms, the *fatigatio* meant a default of vassalic obligations.

39. This refers to the taking of an oath for another legally binding oneself to the validity of the other party's case or to the process by which litigants themselves bolstered the truth of their statements under oath.

40. Besides the land they owned, the *parem bovum* "yoke of oxen" was the most important peasant possession. As such, it was specifically protected by the peace and truce and

50

But concerning the other peasants who are called *bachalarii*,[41] let their oaths be believed up to the amount of four golden mancuses of Valencia.[42] Above this amount, let them prove anything which they swear by the ordeal of boiling water.

51

Let an old knight who cannot defend himself on his own or a poor one who cannot equip himself for judicial battle be believed on oath up to the amount of five golden ounces of Valencia.

52

Let other knights from age twenty to sixty who swear anything about which they are accused of being perjurers defend themselves [in judicial battle] with their own hands against one of equal rank.

53

Let the oaths of burghers be believed as those of knights up to the amount of five golden ounces. Above that amount, let them defend anything they swear by judicial battle; namely, by foot champion.

54

If, in regard to the fiefs which knights hold, their lords deny that they had invested them with these, let the knights show the fiefs to be theirs through oath and judicial battle, and retain possession of them. Let those knights, who do not hold the fiefs and who do not legally claim them, prove either by witnesses or documents that they had acquired these from their lords or else abandon them.

55

If anyone hurls at another a lance, arrow, or any type of weapon, let him make compensation for the wrong done the other person if he wounds him in any way. But if he could not hit him, for the sheer effrontery of having thrown at him, let him await the other person's retaliation under

---

from 1118 was the basic unit for the assessment of a tax, the *bovaticum*, which was ostensibly designed to pay for comital enforcement of rural law and order.

41. The *bachalarii* were wealthy peasants who owned several plots of lands and legally stood between the knights and simple peasants.

42. Gold coin of Valencia first mentioned in Catalonia in 1085.

the same fear or make half of the compensation to him as if he had struck him. And if one while armed seeks out another and does not wound him but only cuts through the shield or armor or makes him dismount or fall to the ground, let him in the same way make half of the compensation as if he had struck him.

56

If anyone kills a horse or any other animal while a man is sitting on it or while holding it with his hand, let him make double compensation for the animal with twice its value and for the dishonor to the rider with an oath.

57

Indeed, let all ships coming to and then returning from Barcelona day and night be under the peace and truce and protection of the prince of Barcelona from Cap de Creus[43] to the port of Salou.[44] And if anyone damages these vessels in any way, let him make double restitution to them through the command of the prince and make amends for his dishonor to the prince with an oath.

58

Likewise, they ruled that all men, noble and ignoble alike, even though they might be mortal enemies, shall be safe for all time day and night and observe a sound truce and true peace from Montcada[45] to Castelldefels[46] from the hill of Finistrel[47] to that of Gavara[48] and from the hill of Erola[49] to the valley of Vitraria[50] and within twelve leagues out to sea. And if anyone disobeys this order in any way, let him make double compen-

43. A rocky headland above the Bay of Roses, the first major landmark of the upper Catalan coast.
44. A small port between Tarragona and Cambrils del Mar best remembered as the staging area for James I's invasion of Majorca in 1229.
45. Castle at the confluence of the Besos River in the western Valles first mentioned in 1022.
46. Village some twenty miles below Barcelona first mentioned in the late tenth century as a settlement surrounding a coastal watchtower.
47. The northernmost limit of Barcelona territory formed by a range of hills to the west of Serola which was in the municipal limit of San Andreu de Palomar.
48. Hill and pass on the north side of the Llobregat River near San Just Desvern.
49. The mountain of Tibidabo to the northwest of Barcelona.
50. Valley to the west of Tibidabo near the Barcelona district of Sarria from where the modern city's finicular railroad originates.

sation for the wrong and dishonor which he has done and pay the prince a hundred golden ounces for the violation of his ban.

59

Roads and thoroughfares on land and sea are the ruler's and, for their protection, must be included in the peace and truce for all days and nights so that all men, both on horseback and on foot, merchants and traders, going and returning on these thoroughfares, may go and return securely and undisturbed without any fear with all their possessions. And if anyone attacks, strikes, wounds, or dishonors them in any way or steals any of their possessions, let him make double compensation to them according to their rank for the wrong and dishonor he has done to their persons; and for what he steals from them, let him make compensation eleven times over. And likewise, let him give the ruler the same amount from his property or fief so, swearing on oath on a holy altar, let him declare that he must make no further compensation for the dishonor he did him.

60

Since a land and its inhabitants are ruined for all time by an evil prince who is without both truth and justice, therefore we the oft-mentioned princes R[amón Berenguer] and A[lmodis], with the counsel and aid of our nobles, decree and command that all princes who will succeed us in this princely office shall have a sincere and perfect faith and truthful speech for all men, noble and ignoble, kings and princes, magnates and knights, peasants and rustics, traders and merchants, pilgrims and way-farers, friends and enemies, Christians and Saracens, Jews and heretics, might trust and believe in the princes without any fear or evil suspicion for their persons but also for their cities and castles, fiefs and property, wives and children, and for anything they possess. And all men, noble and ignoble, magnates, knights, and footmen, sailors, privateers, and minters, who are remaining in their land or coming from elsewhere, should help the aforesaid princes maintain, guard, and govern their faith and true speech in all cases great and small with a righteous faith and without deceit, evil intent or bad counsel. And among other matters, let the peace and promise not to take violent action which the princes should give to Spain and the Saracens on land and sea be maintained by them.

61

In the same way, let the truce and promise not to take violent action which the princes have ordered to be in effect between enemies be rigorously observed, even though these enemies have not confirmed to him the approval of the same truce.

Let no one dare violate the protection[51] which the prince makes in person, through his messenger, *sagio*,[52] or by his seal unless he first prefers charges with the prince in accordance with the custom of his court.

62

Moreover, let both golden and silver coinage be diligently maintained so that it shall in no way increase in copper or decrease in gold or silver nor in weight.

Indeed, whoever infringes, violates, or falsifies all or one of these — namely, the peace and truce, protection, or coinage — cannot make restitution or compensation to the prince since this is such a great wrong and dishonor. Thus to establish this, we order that their persons along with all of their fiefs and property shall come into the ruler's custody for him to do with them as he wishes in accordance with the counsel and approval of his court. Since the faith and justice, peace and truth of the prince, by which all of his realm is ruled, is as strong as the realm and stronger, therefore no one can or must think that restitution or compensation can be made for this by any sum whatsoever. Whoever infringes these abovesaid things cannot make restitution or compensation to the prince unless, as we have ruled above, he shall come into the prince's custody.

63

Likewise, we rule that if anyone shall swear anything to his lord and does not take care to fulfill it, let him make double compensation for any damage which happens to his lord due to the violation of the oath. And if by this payment, he can be in compliance with the oath, thereafter let him observe it and fulfill and complete everything which he had agreed to his lord under oath. However, if he is later found to be a perjurer either let him lose his hand, redeem this penalty with a hundred sous, or lose a fourth of his patrimony, which will come into the possession of the party against whom the perjury was committed. And afterwards let him not testify in court or be believed on oath.

---

51. *Emparamentum* (var. *amparamentum*) connoted protection offered by a lord to his vassals. It could also mean the usurpation of vassalian property under the guise of such lordly protection.

52. A *sagio* (*sayon* Catalan) was a subaltern judicial official who announced tribunals, summoned litigants, took possession of sureties, and saw that verdicts were carried out.

64

Indeed if in any case the prince should be besieged, holds his enemies under siege, or hears that a certain king or prince is coming against him to wage war and he warns his land by both letters and messengers or by the usual customs of warning the land—namely, by bonfires—that it must come to his aid, then let all men, knights and footmen alike, who are old and strong enough to fight come to his aid as quickly as they can immediately after they hear or see the signal. And if one is derelict in giving the prince that which he might render him in this regard, he must lose everything which he holds from him. And he who does not hold a fief from him must make compensation to him for this dereliction of duty and dishonor which he committed against him with his own property and by swearing an oath with his own hands since no man must fail the ruler in such a great matter and crisis.

65

The aforesaid princes further ruled that the holders of *exorchiae*[53]—namely, of the nobles and magnates as well as of the knights and burghers and in all their freeholds—shall come under the control of the princes since that which pleases the prince has the force of law.[54] Moreover, concerning their chattels, let these holders of exorchiae do whatever they wish and bequeath them to relatives, churches, or for their souls.

66

Associations[55] and pacts which knights and footmen mutually make, while wishing to go on military or hunting expeditions, must be rigorously observed by those who hear and sanction them. Concerning those who hear them, remain quiet, and do not oppose them, let them thus have as much profit or loss as was agreed among the others.

67

By a good rule of customary law which was well-sanctioned by all of their vassals, the oft-mentioned princes decreed that no vassals, having

53. An *exorchia* was a feudal or allodial holding of a vassal who died without heirs.

54. The legal maxim *quod principi placuit legis habet vigorem* is a direct quote from Ulpian, *Digest* (I, 4: 1) and Gaius, *Institutes* (I, 4: 1). It became a core of regalist thinking throughout the later Middle Ages.

55. This kind of informal pact among soldiers had a long history springing from the legionary *collegiae* "associations" of Imperial Spain and served as a kind of "rudimentary tontine" by distributing the advantages and dangers of military endeavors among all surviving parties.

lords, for any trick or reason — neither because of a renunciation of fealty, a rupture of ties, nor by the abandonment of their fiefs — shall ambush, pursue, attack, wound, capture, or hold prisoner the persons of their lords. Indeed, if, God forbid!, anyone does this to his lord, let him come under his lord's custody and remain a prisoner until he shall make compensation in accordance with the judgment of the prince and his court to him for the wrong and dishonor committed against him; that is, concerning that wrong which he has committed against the person of his lord.

68[56]

Highways and public roads, flowing water and fresh water springs, meadows and pastures, forests, coppices, and crags existing in this land are the rulers', not so they may have them as a freehold or hold them in lordship but so for all time these shall be for the use of all their people without any hindrance or encroachment and the establishment of any tribute.

Let the rulers hold the crags in such dominion that whoever has them in his fief or freehold shall not build any fortification, castle, church, or monastery on top of or near these without the permission and counsel of the prince. But if anyone who has sworn his fief to the prince and does this, he is to be considered guilty of perjury in this matter until he should abandon this building.

69

We command that the canal of water for the mill which flows to Barcelona shall be intact for all time. And let whoever presumptuously breaks it pay the prince a fine of a hundred golden ounces of Valencia for each instance and let whoever does this secretly for irrigation pay the prince a fine of three of the aforesaid golden ounces for each instance.

70[57]

If anyone lures a baptized Jew or Saracen back to their religion or calls him either "turncoat" or "renegade" or if anyone within our city walls or burghs is the first to draw a sword against another or calls him a

56. This article has strong affinities to the two chapters of the *Libri Feudorum* (II: 5–6; V: 8) which declared that public roads, navigable rivers, ports, mines, and coinage fell under the jurisdiction of the king.

57. This article is similar to a portion of the municipal law code of Tortosa [425] which deals with the uttering of insults between townsmen. It also influenced a law of Jaime I of 1242 which forbade anyone from calling a Jew converted to Christianity *renegat* "renegade," *tornadiz* "turncoat," or *tresallit* "apostate."

"cuckold," let him pay a fine of twenty golden ounces of Valencia to the prince because of his ban. And if he hears or suffers any wrong there, let no compensation be made him for this and afterwards let him await the law and justice of his adversary.

71

By the authority and request of all their nobles, the oft-mentioned princes R[amón Berenguer] and A[lmodis] decreed that all men, noble and ignoble alike, going to, staying with, or returning from the ruler shall have the [protection] of the peace and truce for the whole time, day and night. They shall be unmolested by all their enemies, along with all their fiefs and property as well as all men holding their fiefs, residing on them, or laboring in their service, along with everything which these persons hold and possess, continually until they return to their homes. And if anyone harms anything of theirs or inflicts any damage or commits a crime against them, from that day, he may consider his ties to the ruler broken. And if he suffers any wrong because of this, let no compensation be made him in any way. And let he who disobeys the prince's commands and, for any reason, does any wrong to those placed under this protection or to their possessions, make restitution eleven times over[58] under the constraint of the ruler for all the wrongs which he has committed and everything he has stolen or carried off to those persons against whom he committed these violent acts and afterwards let him make compensation to the ruler for the dishonor he has done him with his own property and by the swearing of an oath with his own hands.

72

They also ruled that, once complaints were made by both sides, if the parties involved in a case afterwards enter into homage, an oath of fealty, or even a pact of friendship by an exchange of good faith and if the aforesaid suits were not maintained, they shall be perpetually null and void and considered terminated.

73

Indeed, let none of the magnates — namely, the viscounts, *comitores*, or *vasvassores* — hereafter presume in any way to either punish crimi-

58. This level of compensation was an extremely harsh one in comparison with the early Catalan peace and truce or with other articles of the *Usatges* which seldom exceeded double compensation (*in duplum*). Elevenfold compensation, though enacted in the *Liber Judiciorum* (VIII, I, 6; IX, 2, 5) for robbery or recruiting violations, was even relatively rare in Visigothic law.

nals (that is, to hang them for justice) or to build a new castle against the prince, or hold his fortification under siege or wage war with siege engines which are vulgarly called *fundibula*, *goza*, and *gata*[59] since this is a great dishonor to the rulers. But if a person does this, let him abandon or destroy the castle or give it back to the prince without any lessening of its value if he had captured it, immediately after being so demanded by the prince. And by the distraint of the prince, let him make double compensation for all offenses he has committed there to the person against whom he committed them. And if he captures knights and other vassals there, let him release and return them to the prince. Indeed, let him afterwards make compensation to him for the dishonor which he has done him in this matter with his property or fief by swearing an oath with his own hands but he is not bound to make any further compensation to him. Thus the exercise of this distraint is conceded to none but the rulers.

Since the rendering of justice in regard to criminals — namely, concerning murderers, adulterers, sorcerers, robbers, rapists, traitors, and other men — is granted only to the rulers, thus let them render justice as it seems fit to them: by cutting off hands and feet, putting out eyes, keeping men in prison for a long time and, ultimately, in hanging their bodies if necessary

In regard to women, let the rulers render justice: by cutting off their noses, lips, ears, and breasts, and by burning them at the stake if necessary, And since a land cannot live without justice, therefore it is granted to the rulers to render justice. And just as it is granted to them to render justice, thus it is permissible for them to release and pardon whomever they please.

74[60]

Let all offenses committed during the truce of the Lord always be doubly compensated, except for those persons who are ejected from the peace and truce of the Lord.

75

Let a truce given between friends and enemies be observed and maintained without deceit for all time. Indeed, if, God forbid! it is violated in any way, let simple restitution be made.

76

The oft-mentioned princes ruled concerning all men except

---

59. The *fundibula* and *gussa* were catapults of various sizes and designs. The *gatta* was a battering ram.

60. This article has strong ties to the peace laws of Ausona and Barcelona in 1064.

knights — that is, burghers, bailiffs, and peasants — that their lords, in whose fiefs they were when they were killed or suffered any wrong or affront to their persons, fiefs, or property, shall receive a third of the compensation if because of this their lord comes to their aid. Nevertheless, with the approval and counsel of the good men or through the judgment of the ruler and his land, let them make a judicial settlement with those from whom they receive the compensation.

77

If one suffers any wrong, and, before he seeks vengeance for it, consequently seeks justice and if the malefactor promises to render justice to him and he [the victim], refusing it, afterwards commits another crime, first let him make compensation for the wrong which he has committed and afterwards let him then receive justice from the malefactor from whom justice must then be rendered him. But if the malefactor resists justice and he afterwards suffers any wrong, let no compensation be made him in any way.

78

Likewise, the aforesaid princes decreed that rulers shall confirm and maintain for all time the peace and truce of the Lord, and act to have it confirmed and maintained by the magnates and knights of the land, as well as all men living in their country. And if anyone violates the peace and truce of the Lord in any way, he must make restitution according to the judgment of the bishops.

79

If anyone has vassals who, without his order or consent, commit any wrong to another and he promises to render justice between them and the other parties and he wishes to post a surety so that he should act to render justice and if he who has suffered the crime does not want to receive justice and thereafter commits some crime to any of the vassals, first, let him make restitution just as it was judged for the crime he has committed and then let him receive justice from the lord for his vassals just as a lord is bound to render it for them. Thus just as a reprisal committed because of a deprivation of justice[61] must in no way remain in effect, so compensation shall not be made.

---

61. Unlike the *fatigatio de directo* in which a person would not submit to justice at all or not accept the work of a legitimate tribunal, the *proferimentum de directo* was any willful delay

80[62]

If a person has any grievance against another and summons him to render justice, and he, for the fear of God, nor by an order of a judge, nor by the advice of relatives and friends, wants to render justice to the plaintiff and the plaintiff, moved by anger, steals his chattels, burns down his houses, destroys his standing crops, vines, and trees, and then at any times afterwards the defendant comes to justice, first, let him make restitution for any damage he has done to the plaintiff and for the profit which he might have garnered from the plaintiff's possessions, and then let the plaintiff give back any of the defendant's possessions he might have. But indeed if any of these possessions were consumed, let him restore as much profit as he garnered to the present time and afterwards let the defendant render justice to the plaintiff, as is obligatory and fitting for him to do.

81

If anyone is proven guilty and convicted of homicide, let him come into the custody of the deceased's next-of kin and their lord. If he does not want to or cannot render justice, they can do what they wish with him, short of his death.

82

Concerning the compensation for all men who were killed, their sons or relatives, from whom a legitimate succession is fitting for the claim of inheritance, could charge the defendant or murderer, and undoubtedly have the right to take vengeance on him. But if they do this, let them have the compensation for homicide just as it was decreed to be done concerning defendants or murderers according to the laws[63] or the customs of their land.

83

Concerning bailiffs of whatever sort, they must be legally answerable for their lords and their rights by the ordeal of boiling water, even in

---

of litigation by one of the litigants who had preferred charges before a tribunal but hoped to delay its work as long as possible. It is the direct opposite of the form *facere directum* which signified that a person was willing to carry out his judicial responsibilities.

62. This article is drawn almost exclusively from the southern French legal collection, the *Petri Exceptiones* (IV, 17).

63. The compensations for homicide in the *Liber Judiciorum* (*LV*, VI, 1, 2–5; VIII, 4, 16; IX, 2, 3) fall into two categories: (1) those committed by "malicious intent" or "gross" negligence which called for fines payable to the Crown ranging from 300 to 500 solidi (the gold coinage of the Visigothic realm) and (2) those occasioned by less blatant negligence which were settled by the payment of smaller sums to the next-of-kin.

matters not involving judgements. Indeed let no bailiff grant his bailiwicks to his heirs without his lord's consent.

84

If a peasant takes back that which was rightfully confiscated from him,[64] let him give five sous for the sheer effrontery. And if he takes anything except within his rights, let him make double restitution in this case. Let a knight who takes such things pay back and restore exactly what he has taken along with an oath.

85

If anyone violently rapes a virgin, either let him marry her if she and her parents are willing and let them give her dowry[65] to him or let him give her a husband equal to his rank. If one violently ravishes a women who is not a virgin and makes her pregnant, let him do the same.

86

Concerning the possessions and patrimony of childless peasants or holder (*exorchii*) who have departed from this world, let their lords have the same portion which the sons would have if any sons procreated by the exorchii had survived.

87

Likewise concerning the possessions and property of adulteresses if the adultery is committed against the husband's will, let them and their lords have equal portions of all the adulterous wives' property. But if, God forbid! this adultery is committed with the will, order, or assent of the husbands, let their lords have full right and jurisdiction in such cases.

88

However, if the women do not carry this out by their free will but from the fear or order of their husbands, let them be exempt from the

---

64. The *disemparamentum* was the opposite of the *emperamentum*, the lordly confiscation of the feudal tenure of a vassal derelict in his service. The *disemperamentum* thus consisted of the vassals' illegal seizure of the confiscated holding.

65. The *exovar* had become one of the most prevalent dotarial forms in Catalonia during the period of the Usatges compilation. It derived from the Arabic *al-ashwwar*, the bride's household furniture and cooking implements, but by the end of the twelfth century the *exovar* had become synonymous with the Latin *dos* "dowry" in describing grants exchanged between a bethrothed couple or from the parents of the bride to their future son-in-law.

actions of their husbands and their [husbands'] lords and not subject to the loss of any of their own property. And if these same women desire it, they may separate from their husbands and yet nevertheless let them not lose their dowry or wedding gift.

89[66]

Husbands can accuse their wives of adultery or even of the suspicion of it and then they must clear themselves by their affirmation on oath and by judicial battle if there are clear indications and evident signs in these. Moreover, wives of knights should do so by oath and likewise by judicial battle between knights. Wives of townsmen and burghers and noble bailiffs, by judicial battle between foot champions. Wives of peasants, by their own hands through the ordeal of boiling water. If the wife is victorious, let her husband honorably keep her and make compensation to her for all expenses which her retainers have incurred in this suit and judicial battle. But if she is defeated, let her come into the custody of her husband with everything she has.

90

A true informer will not be so considered unless that which he informs about he demonstrates as true by oath, judicial battle, or judgement by boiling or freezing water.

91

No one can encumber, defend, or retain as his own jurisdiction that which is under the jurisdiction of sanctuaries or is owned by the rulers or is within the boundaries of castles, even if possessed for a period of two hundred years.

92

Let guardians and bailiffs be legally answerable for their wards if these are willing. But if, however, they are not, this must wait until the ward shall come of age; that is, twenty years old, so they may engage in litigation with plaintiffs. But if these plaintiffs can prove that they were deprived of justice by the wards' fathers, from then on the guardians must be legally answerable and engage in litigation for the wards without any delay. How-

---

66. This article is drawn from a passage of the *Liber Judiciorum LV*, III, 4, 3) on adulteresses.

ever, when a father thus dies, let his vassals immediately come before his son even if he is a small child, become his vassals by commending themselves with their own hands, accept from his hand the castles and fiefs which they held by the grant of his father, and give him control of these castles. Then let them go with him to the lord under whose authority he must hold his fief and commend himself to him and accept from his hand the fief which his father held for him. Let the vassals with the guardian, and the guardian with them serve the Lord. So indeed the ward should not lose his fief, let the guardian's vassals make a sure act of fealty to the lord. Yet indeed if the guardian wishes to diminish the ward's fief or keep it longer than the usual period, let these vassals help their lord without deceit. In the meanwhile, let the guardian truly take charge of the boy and his fief and raise him well and honorably, make him a knight when he reaches a fitting age and return his fief to him. But if, however, the ward is a girl, let the guardian provide her with a husband with the advice and counsel of the good men, and likewise return her fief to her without diminution. Let peasants from age fifteen recover their fiefs and chattels.

93[67]

After Saracens have run away, let whoever finds and keeps them in custody before they should cross the Llobregat return them to their masters and have as his reward one *mancus*[68] for each. From the Llobregat to the Francoli, three-and-a-half *mancuses*. Past that, one ounce as well as their chains and clothing.

94

If a peasant finds either gold or silver, which in the vernacular is called *bonas*,[69] a horse or mule, a Saracen or goshawk, let him immediately notify his lord, show and return it to him, and then receive whatever reward his lord wishes to give him.

67. This article has affinities to a passage of the *Liber Judiciorum* (*LV*, IX, 1, 4) on fugitive slaves.

68. A golden coin of the Caliphate of Cordoba which circulated in both Muslim and Christian Iberian territory throughout the eleventh century. It was imitated by the moneyers of Berenguer Ramón I and Ramón Berenguer I. This Christian *mancus* circulated from 1019 to the last decade of Ramón Berenguer I's life.

69. *Bonas* was a vernacular term used to describe deposits of precious minerals or coin hoards.

95

When a peasant suffers injury to the body or damage to his property or fief, let him in no way dare take vengeance or settle the dispute but as soon as he suffers the wrong, then let him make an end to this matter in accordance with his lord's command.

96

At times, we have ordered that the sous to be used for the payment of the fine for cutting down trees be golden as the law prescribes,[70] and at other times in dinars. Just as all trees do not have the same value, thus they must not bear an equal fine [for the felling of them]. And we allow that this fine may increase or decrease according to the ruling of a judge. Indeed, let this fine be made according to the value of the trees and the damage and dishonor to their owners.

97

In a bailiwick or castle guardianship for which one has done homage or paid tribute, if one guards and defends this to the best of his ability, he must have judicial rights[71] and a moderate utilization — namely, of grass, straw, gardens, and fruits of trees — nor must any wrong come to him there for any reason. But if it does, let the lord of the freehold make compensation to him, and, if he has a suit or war because of this bailiwick or castle guardianship, likewise let the lord help him. Concerning a bailiwick or castle guardianship for which one has not done homage or tribute, he will not have judicial rights but will have all the rest.

98

If anyone claims he was deprived of justice from the prince, a bishop, his lord, or his adversary in a legal suit, or alleges that he was ejected from the peace and truce of the Lord by one of them, or says that his lord has broken feudal ties with him, and cannot prove it, let him make compensation for all offenses which he has committed in this case. Afterwards, let

70. The passage referred to is VII, 3, 1 of the *Liber Judiciorum* which lays out a detailed schedule for the unlawful felling of various types of trees.

71. The *estaticum* was a set of judicial rights that included the assessing of fines, the forcing of litigants to abide by verdicts and settlements, and even the carrying out of capital punishment. The bailiff or castellan exercised these rights over the population of the castle and its territory and yet had to relinquish these rights whenever the lord reclaimed the *potestas* of the fortress or tenure.

him file suit, seek justice, demand adjudication, and thus do so publicly so often that it cannot be denied him.

99

Let all vassals maintain the peace and truce with the rulers for thirty days after they have broken feudal ties with them; let the rulers maintain it with their viscounts and *comitores* for fifteen days; and with the vasvasours and other knights, for ten days.

100

Let Christians not sell weapons to the Saracens except with the consent of the prince. But if they do so, let them reclaim the weapons which they have sold, no matter how difficult for them. And unless they do so, let them pay the ruler a fine of a hundred golden ounces.

101

Let them pay the same fine if they sell food to them contrary to the prince's wishes.

102

Let a person who informs the Saracens concerning a military expedition or strategy of the ruler or who betrays his plans or secrets pay the same fine, after he has made compensation for any wrong which takes place because of this.

103

Indeed, the above-mentioned princes issued another noble, honorable, and useful rule of customary law which they observed and commanded their successors to perpetually observe — namely, that they shall maintain a court and a great household, form a band of retainers, give them soldier's fees,[72] grant redress, render justice, judge according to the law, support the oppressed, and come to the aid of the besieged. And that whenever the princes want to eat, they should have the horn blown so the nobles and commoners will come to dine and there the princes should

---

72. The *sollata* (var. *solidata*) was a royal grant, usually of money, not unlike the northern European fief-rent. This stipend, originally of no more than one sou, compensated vassals who were forced to spend more than the customary term in the sovereign's host or those in the martial employ of lords other than their own.

distribute fine garments which they have among the magnates and within their own household, and there summon military expeditions with whom they set out to destroy Spain, and there make new knights.

104

Likewise, the oft-mentioned princes ruled that if anyone in person or through messenger wishes to break feudal ties with his lord, he may be secure in doing this; secure while he comes, secure while he stays, and secure until he returns home. But, in the meanwhile, if he knows of damage to his lord, he should prevent it if he can. But if he cannot, he should notify his lord about it and, unless he does so, he will bear the fault for the damage done by the malefactor.

105

They also ruled that if parents with sons or sons with parents have a legal dispute or lawsuit, let the fathers be judged as lords and the sons as vassals who have commended themselves with their own hands.

106

But if sons commit any crime against the lord of their fathers, let the fathers force their sons to make restitution and compensation to their lords for this crime or let the fathers themselves make compensation for them. But if they do not want to do this, let the fathers totally disinherit their sons and abandon their support of them without deceit.

107

Likewise, they ruled that if any son of a magnate of the land, whether of greater or lesser status, did any wrong to any vassal of his father's castle or his fief or with his own vassals, the father should himself force his son or his vassals holding his land to make restitution for the wrong they have done or he should make restitution for them. Yet if the son besides does any wrong to another person from other places and not from his father's castle or from his fiefs nor with his father's vassal, neither should he return to the paternal castle or fief nor should his father or mother do him any favor nor protect him in anything. But if they do, they should make compensation for the wrong their son and the vassals he leads with him have committed.

108

Indeed, the aforesaid princes also decreed that if a dispute occurs or a lawsuit arises between Christians and Jews, two witnesses from both parties — namely, one from the Christian and the other from the Jew — shall suffice to prove their cases. Thus nevertheless if the case is to be proved for the Christians, both witnesses should testify and the Jew swear an oath. And if it is to be proved for the Jew, likewise they should both testify and the Christian should swear an oath.

109

The aforesaid princes ruled and acknowledged it to be good faith that no men, after they have greeted or kissed each other, shall commit any crime against the other person on that day. But if, God forbid! they did this, they should make restitution and compensation without any interdict to the person against whom they have committed this crime.

110

Indeed, they likewise established and approved as sound judgement that if anyone enjoys another's hospitality and dines with him, he shall completely abstain from doing any damage whatsoever to him for the next seven days nor, by any kind of artifice, commit any crime against him in any way or for any reason either through his lord, retainer, or in person. But if it happens that he should do this, he shall make restitution and compensation against the one who has done this.

111

Therefore they ruled that if anyone traveled with another, or was with him either on the road, in his home, a field or in any other place and if another person then attacks him or wants to take any of his things from him, his companion should help him against all men as best as he can without deceit, even against his own lords, and he shall fear no official charge because of this. And his lord may not then file suit in any way against him concerning any part of his homage or for the violation of his oath, unless he was warned beforehand by his lord or his lord's retainer that he should not guide nor accompany the person.

112[73]

Then the aforesaid princes, being at Barcelona at the Church of the Holy Cross and Saint Eulalia the Martyr, with the counsel and aid of their bishops — namely, Berenguer of Barcelona, Guillem of Ausona, and Berenguer of Gerona, as well as the abbots and the monastic clergy of different orders and with the assent and acclamation of the magnates of their land and other God-fearing Christians — confirmed the peace and truce of the Lord and decreed that it be observed in their land for all time. And if it was violated in any way, restitution and compensation shall be made as it has been committed to writing at this time in each see and bishopric of their land.

113

If a person who has posted a guaranty refuses to carry out the obligation[74] he agreed to, it is permissible for the person against whom the obligation was broken to compel and distrain him within the limits of the peace and truce forever. But he nevertheless should practice a moderate distraint and make a fitting guaranty since it is not just to take great guaranties for moderate debts. Yet if the person who posted the guaranty carries out his obligation and pays the debt from his own funds and the person who imposed this guaranty on him does not want to release him from it, let him be forced to pay this debt twice over to the guarantor for all the damage which has happened to him because of this guaranty.

114

If anyone slights his lord, basely answers him and lies in an accusation against him and therefore the vassal suffers any wrong because of this, let no compensation be made him in any way if the lord was telling the truth concerning this. But, however, if the lord was lying concerning this, let him therefore compensate his vassal for the wrong and dishonor which has then happened to him in this matter.

---

73. This article is a close approximation of the prologue of the Barcelona *pax et treuga* of 1064.

74. The phrase *portare fidem* in this case signifies the complex of mutual obligations between lord and vassal and emphasizes the ties of *bona fide* "good faith" between the two.

115

Indeed, after a knight is accused of treason by his lord, he must not be legally answerable for his lord in other suits until he shall be cleared of this accusation unless the lord releases him of the accusation beforehand.

116

The oft-mentioned princes also ruled that if persons of greater rank have a suit with those of lesser rank and an oath was directed to be taken between them, let the greater swear in person with the lesser if the lesser can have men of rank equal to the greater to swear for them. But if not, however, the lesser shall swear with the greater and the greater provide them men of equal rank and these shall swear to them what the men of greater rank have to swear. But if all of this is impossible for them, let oaths be made from each party by individuals who are Christians and their vassals, having commended themselves with their own hands. They likewise decreed this for common suits, in which no one holds lordship or suzerainty.

117

Concerning those who depart this world intestate, if they leave wives and children, let their lords accede to a third of their patrimony. And if they leave children and no wives, let the aforesaid lords accede to a half. If wives and no children, let the aforesaid lords accede to half and the relatives of the deceased, the other half. But if the relatives are dead, after the rights of the wives have been observed in all places, let it all be given to the lords. Thus exactly what is proclaimed above for men shall be in effect concerning intestate wives.

118[75]

By the authority and request of all their noble and magnates, the oft-mentioned princes R[amón Berenguer] and A[lmodis] ruled that every grant shall remain permanently unrepealed and in effect. In addition, if anyone wants to grant his castle, fief, or any possession to his son or daughter, nephew or niece, indeed he shall do so under the following condition: that he shall retain possession of everything he has granted for all the days of his life, and, after his death, everything shall revert to the person to whom he had granted it. And he agrees to abide by the following

75. This article shows the influence of a passage of the *Liber Judiciorum* (V, 2, 6) on written donations.

stipulation: that he may in no way change his will—namely, that he shall receive the heir as a vassal commended by his own hands, or grant him control of a castle, or commend the castellan of the castle as well as those who hold the fief which he has granted him as vassals or make him establish lawful possession of the aforesaid castle and fief from the lord from whose authority the granter holds the same castle or fief. But if he does all or one of the aforementioned things, then he cannot change his will if this grant was justly made or no other legal cause impedes it. For the laws and decrees allow a father to endow his son or nephew, granting to or benefitting him from his own estate.[76] And it is sometimes customary to do this openly and sometimes secretly due to the fear from other sons, lords, or even from relatives and retainers. Therefore, the aforesaid princes and all of their court approved with a wholesome intent and, with this approval, ruled that the aforesaid mode of tenure [namely; homage, control of a castle, commendation of a castellan, or establishment of lawful possession from a lord] attain such a validity that this cannot be subverted or changed by any fraudulence and trickery or through any deceit. In this way and manner, a father and grandfather can endow his son or daughter or even his nephew or niece.

119[77]

The aforesaid forebears, however, can disinherit their sons or daughters, nephews or nieces if they act with such effrontery as to seriously strike or dishonor their fathers, mothers, grandfathers or grandmothers, accuse them of a crime before a tribunal, or if the sons become traitors, or the daughters do not want to marry husbands but live shamefully, or if the sons become Saracens and do not want to recant. If indeed they have been clearly proven guilty of such things, they must be expelled from their inheritance from the abovementioned persons, if the grandfathers or grandmothers, fathers or mothers are willing.

120[78]

If anyone wishes to disinherit his son or daughter, nephew or niece, let him do so by name and state the wrongful act for which he is disinheriting him, establish another heir in this place, and let the case of

76. This section of the article is drawn from a passage of the *Liber Judiciorum* (IV, 2, 18) dealing with the inheritance of infants who die shortly after baptism.
77. This article is a reworking of IV, 5, 1 of the *Liber Judiciorum* and I, 15 of the *Petri Exceptiones*, both of which deal with the disinheritance of children.
78. This article was influenced by 1, 18 of the *Petri Exceptiones* which outlines the four conditions in which disinheritance is allowed.

disinheritance be proven by the person established as the true heir. If any of these things are not done, a person can in no way disinherit his son or daughter, nephew or niece. And if he presumes to do so, this action will be null and void.

121

Princes, magnates, and knights can likewise give their fiefs to whomever they wish — namely, in regard to that fief to which they should expect to accede by an act of reversion[79] after the death of any possessor [of the fief]. But afterwards they cannot change their decision if the recipient was already one of their vassals commended with their own hands or, because of this grant, they received him as a vassal. If this tenure is such for him and his lord denies that he had given him this fief, a formal verification shall be sufficient for him to act as if he had already held the fief. Therefore, very often this grant was found to have been done in secret. Moreover, the oft-mentioned princes gave verification to such a grant for all times.

122

Let a judgment rendered in court by a judge chosen from the court be accepted by all and be in force for all time. Let no one by any artifice or trickery dare to refuse to obey it. But whoever does this or wishes to do so shall come personally, along with everything he is considered to own, into the custody of the prince so he may do as he wishes with him since he who refuses the judgement of the court, attacks the veracity of the court; and he who attacks the veracity of the court, harms the prince. And he who wishes to harm the prince should be punished and condemned for all time along with his progeny since one is demented and senseless who wishes to resist or stand in opposition to the wisdom and experience of the court in which there are princes, bishops, counts, viscounts, *comitores*, *vasvasssores*, learned and wise men, and judges.

123

The judgments of the court and the rules of customary law must be freely accepted and observed, since they were only issued because of the

79. The *aperecio* (var. *apertura*, *adoberta*) described the condition of a feudal tenure at the death of its current holder when it became *apertus* "vacant" and reverted to the lord's authority for disposition. While it was in the purview of lordly power to grant vacant fiefs to whomever it wished, the tenure normally went to the deceased vassal's descendant.

severity of the law, in that, everybody can file suit according to the law but not everyone can carry out all compensation in accordance with it[80] which judges that homicide is to be compensated by three hundred golden *solidi*[81] which is worth four thousand fine silver sous; the putting out of an eye, by a hundred; the cutting off a hand, by a hundred; of a foot, by a hundred; and the same for other members of body. Of course, they judge all men equally and indeed rule noting [relations] between vassal and lord. Since these things must be done or were done in accordance with the rules of customary law, the aforesaid princes ruled that all judgments shall be rendered according to the rules of customary law, and when the rules of customary law are not sufficient, let the laws, the ruling of the prince, and the judgment of his court be reverted to.

124[82]

If anyone lies in ambush during the truce of God, or arranges for an ambush within the fief or the boundaries of his enemy's castle and commits a crime through this ambush on the day after the truce ends, he therefore must make compensation as if he had done it during the truce of the Lord.

125[83]

The above-mentioned princes ruled that everyone shall wait for his adversary until the third hour of the day [nine A.M.]. Indeed, then if he so wishes, let him take possession of the pledges and consider this failure to appear to be a deprivation of justice if the adversary himself who has failed to come to the tribunal does not consider himself to be without deceit. And if he does retain them, he may not demand the suit's adjudication through his advocate. This is not so between vassals and their lords — it seems fitting that vassals wait for their lords until the ninth hour [three P.M.].

80. The table of compensation mentioned in this article comes from VI, 4, 3 of the *Liber Judiciorum*.

81. Gold coin (*solidus aureus*) first issued by Constantine I in 310 and imitated in form by the kings of Visigothic Spain.

82. This article is drawn from passages of the peace and truce laws of Ausona and Barcelona in 1064 concerning the setting of ambushes during or shortly after the Lord's truce.

83. This article is drawn from II, 1, 17 of the *Liber Judiciorum* which allowed for a conclusion of suits by judges only or by judge and advocate.

Text Appendix One

A1

Let no one taken prisoner by a court and interned in a castle as a verdict then leave it without permission. But if he presumes to do so, except perhaps for fear of death, he will pay the penalty for assault[84]; that is, thirty sous, which he will give to the court. Then after he has returned to the castle, let him make compensation for the guilt he has incurred as the court judges.

A2

The oft-mentioned princes also ruled and ordered that all men living in their country shall for all time make peace and war by sea and land with the Saracens according to the princes' orders.

A3

The oft-mentioned princes R. and A., along with their magnates, also approved and sanctioned that bishops, in their chapters or synods, also in their councils or communities, shall investigate, judicially intercede, punish, and judge churches and clerics as well as their rights and jurisdictions, along with all infractions of the peace and sacrilege committed in their bishoprics

Text Appendix Two

B1[85]

Let whoever kills a subdeacon pay a fine of three hundred sous; a deacon, four hundred sous; a priest, six hundred sous. Let whoever is judged guilty of killing a monk pay a fine of four hundred sous; a bishop, nine hundred sous.

B2[86]

We command that in order to have perjury prevented, witnesses shall not be admitted to take an oath before they have been interrogated.

---

84. This penalty of thirty solidi is drawn from VIII, 1, 4 of *Liber Judiciorum*.

85. This article is drawn verbatim from a canon of the Council of Clermont of 1095.

86. This article is based on the capitulary of Charlemagne issued in 805 (*Capitulare missorum in Theodonis villa*) on judicial proceedings.

And if they cannot be interrogated otherwise, they shall be isolated and individually questioned. And it shall not be permissible for a plaintiff to summon witnesses when the defendant is absent. And generally no one except those who have been isolated shall be admitted to take an oath or give testimony. And if one is admitted to give testimony and is refused, let the person who refuses him say so and demonstrate why he does not want to admit him. Let witnesses be selected from this territory and from none other, unless the case must be investigated farther than the boundaries of the county. And if one was convicted of perjury, let him lose his land or redeem it with a hundred sous.

B3 [87]

And before witnesses may be interrogated concerning a case, let them be constrained to swear an oath that they would say nothing other than the truth. We also order that more honorable [of higher status] witnesses shall be given more credibility than that of less honorable ones. The testimony of one person, no matter how well-placed and worthy of belief, must in no way be considered.

B4 [88]

If when an unjust appeal was proven of anyone, let him be constrained to reimburse the expenses which his adversary had to bear for the appeal not simply once but four times over. Two or three credible witnesses are sufficient to prove all suits; the testimony of only one is condemned by the laws and canons.

B5 [89]

Let no one ever presume to be plaintiff, judge, and witness at the same time since it is necessary for four persons to always be present in every tribunal; that is, the chosen judges, credible plaintiffs, fit defendants, and witnesses worthy of belief. Moreover, judges must act with fairness; plain-

87. The ultimate origin of this passage is II, 39, 3 of the Theodosian Code (*De fide testium et instrumentorum*). It was then transmitted through the *Breviary of Alaric* (II, 14, 2), the *Liber Judiciorum* (II, 14, 2), and the *Decretum* (XVI: 204) and *Panormia* (V: 21) of Ivo of Chartres.

88. The first section of this article is drawn from a passage of the *Breviary of Alaric* (XI, 2, 14) which was itself a citation from a law manual of the early Republic, the *Sententiae Petrii* (5, 39, 1). The second section is drawn from the *Pauli Exceptiones* (4, 30).

89. The earliest source of this article is a capitulary of Charlemagne issued in 744. It later appeared in Ivo's *Panormia* (IV, 81) and Gratian's *Decretum* (case IV, question 4, chapter 1).

tiffs, with the intention of amplifying the case; the defendants, with the intention of narrowing the case by putting limits on it; and witnesses must prove the truth.

B6[90]

Those who were enemies the day before or shortly before cannot be plaintiffs or witnesses so that they, in anger, should not desire to cause harm or take vengeance. There an unobstructed, uninfluenced, and believable will of the plaintiffs and witnesses must be sought. Let those who seem capable of being commanded by the parties for whom they appear as witnesses not be considered credible witnesses.

B7[91]

Let no accusation be lodged against anyone in writing, but let one make an accusation in his own voice if he is to be a credible and fit plaintiff; clearly, let the person he had wished to accuse be present since no one can accuse or be accused while absent.

Text Appendix Three

C1

We indeed command that if any freeholder, knight, or peasant wishes to grant or sell his freehold to a church, monastery, or any person, let him — except for bailiffs of nobles — have permission to do so and be in as full a possession of the freehold as the men living then or in the future.

C2

The said princes ruled that if a lord confiscates from a bailiff his bailiwick because of his failure to render justice and the bailiff in any way usurps this jurisdiction from his lord, he shall lose the bailiwick and make compensation from his own funds to his lord for this dishonor if he remained with his lord in any other office. And after he made a reimbursal from his own funds if his lord can prove in any tribunal how much was

90. The first part of this article is a citation from Ivo's *Decretum* (V, 239) and *Panormia* (IV, 1, 34) and Gratian's *Decretum* (c.III, q. 5, c.2). The second section is a quotation from the *Digest* (22, 5, 16) which was also cited in Ivo's *Decretum* (XVI, 181) and *Panormia* (V, 33) and Gratian's *Decretum* (c. II, q. 8, c. 5).
91. This article is drawn from Ivo's *Decretum* (VI, 328) and *Panormia* (IV, 53).

embezzled by him, let him make compensation nine times over and then he should not cross through the bailiwick unless his lord wished it.

C3

If anyone produces in a tribunal a document or charter validated on oath concerning any lawsuit in court and the case of the other party cannot be proven either by witnesses or validated documents, let the judge rule what seems right to him and let each party observe his verdict.

C4[92]

If a widow lives honorably and chastely after the death of her husband in his fief in raising her children well, let her possess her husband's estate as long as she remains without a husband. But if she commits adultery and violates her husband's marriage bed, let her lose the fief and let all the property of her husband come under the control of her sons if they are of age or under the control of their relatives. Thus, nevertheless, let her not lose her own property [if it currently seems to be hers] or her dowry as long as she shall live and afterwards let it revert to her sons or relatives.

C5

If anyone mortgages the bailiwick or fief of his lord without his consent, the lord can rightfully confiscate it whenever he wishes. Indeed if he knows about this and does not oppose it, he may not confiscate it but the bailiff shall post a surety with him according to the value of the bailiwick or fief and make compensation since he did not take action with the lord's advice but by having contempt for it.

C6

If after a lord, who is in need for any reason, has demanded service or any aid from his bailiff or a vassal holding his fief and is refused, and if after once, twice, and again repeating [his demand], he [the bailiff or vassal] refuses to carry out the service or aid, let him post a surety to the best of his ability to his lord, make double compensation for the first demanded compensation for the first demanded service which the lord sought, and not refuse his aid any longer.

---

92. This article is a combination of two passages of the *Liber Judiciorum* (IV, 2, 16) on the division of a deceased husband's property and (III, 2, 1) on sexual improprieties of a widow and the legal repercussions for such acts.

C7

If anyone accepts another's vassal giving him any soldier's pay for defense, he [the soldier] is not obliged to come to his aid in the customary way vassals are to do for their lord.

C8[93]

The ancients customarily called a castle, a fortress situated on a very high place, as if it were a high house. Its plural is castra amd diminutive castellum.

Text Appendix Four

D1[94]

Each nation chooses its own law from custom. Indeed, a long-established custom arises in place of law. Law, however, is a species of justice. Indeed usage and long-established custom are equally derived from usages. However, custom is a certain right founded on usages which arises in place of law. Indeed, what a king or emperor decrees is therefore called a decree or edict. Moreover, all justice is established from laws and usages, Indeed, a usage is a custom approved by long duration. The establishment of equity is twofold: at times in the laws and at others in the usages.

D2[95]

Moreover, privileges are laws of individuals just as if they are private laws; for, a privilege is likewise so called because it exists on a private level.

---

93. This is an exact citation from Isidore's *Etymologiae* (XV, 2, 13).
94. This is a combination of two passages from the *Etymologiae* (II, 10, 1; V, 3, 2–3).
95. This is a citation of V, 18 of the *Etymologiae*.

Appendix I: Catalan Peace and Truce Laws Prior to the *Usatges*

I: Comital Peace Assembly of Barcelona — 1064[1]

In the year of our Lord 1064, a confirmation of the peace or pact of the Lord was made by the bishops, namely, Berenguer of Barcelona, Guillem of Ausona, and Berenguer of Gerona as well as the abbots, the religious clerics of each order at Barcelona in the church of the see of the Holy Cross by the order of the princes, the Lord Ramón and Lady Almodis of Barcelona, with the assent and acclamation of the magnates of their land and other God-fearing Christians.

　1. Indeed, by the constitution of the aforesaid bishops and princes, it was enacted that from this day hereafter no person of either sex shall violate or invade either a church or dwellings which are or will be within a circle of thirty paces [one hundred and fifty feet] around the church except the bishop or canons to whom this church is subject on account of its rent or to eject an excommunicated person from it. Yet we do not place under this protection those churches in which fortifications are built. Indeed, we order that those churches in which robbers or thieves put booty or stolen goods or from which they leave or to which they return while committing offenses, shall be unmolested until charges concerning the offense are preferred before the church's own bishop or before the see of Barcelona. If however, these robbers or thieves do not want to undergo justice according to the order of the bishop or canons of the see of Barcelona or postpone it, then by the authority of the bishop of the aforesaid see and the canons, let this church be considered without immunity. Moreover, let one who otherwise violates a church or attacks whatever is within a circle of thirty paces around it make restitution with the sum of six-hundred sous for the sacrilege and let him be subject to excommunication until he shall suitably make compensation.

1. Fita, "Cortes y usajes," 389–93.

2. Likewise it was resolved that no person shall assault clerks who are not bearing arms, monks, nuns, and other women or those traveling with bishops if they are not bearing arms. Indeed, let no person violate a community of canons or monks or steal anything from there.

3. Likewise the aforesaid bishops and princes confirmed that no person in this bishopric of Barcelona shall make plunder of horses or their foals, male or female mules, cattle, male or female asses, sheep, or goats. Indeed, let no man burn or destroy the dwellings of peasants or clergy who are not bearing arms except for those properties in which knights live. Let no person dare seize or distrain a male or female villager or extort money from them. Let no one burn or cut standing crops, cut down an olive tree, or remove their fruits. Indeed let no one pour out another's wine.

4. Moreover, whoever violates this peace which we have proclaimed and does not make compensation with the sum of the fine within fifteen days to the person against whom he violated it, let him make double compensation if the fifteen days have passed.

5. Moreover, the aforesaid bishops strongly confirmed the pact of the Lord, which the people call *treuga* (truce); namely, from the first day of the Advent of the Lord to the octave of the Epiphany of the Lord and from the Monday preceeding Ash Wednesday to the first Monday after the octave of Pentecost Sunday and in the three vigils as well as the feasts of Holy Mary,[2] indeed the vigils and feasts of the Twelve Apostles and also the vigils and feasts of the martyrs Saint Eulalia and Saint Cugat of Barcelona and also the vigils of the two feasts of Christmas and the Holy Cross. We also placed these feasts with their vigils; namely, those of Saint John the Baptist, Saint Lawrence, Saint Michael the Archangel, Saint Martin, and All Saints Day under this observance of religion.[3] And they similarly placed under such an observance the vigils of the same [All Saints Day] and fast days of the four seasons.

6. The aforesaid bishops not only confirmed that the aforesaid feast days are in the truce of the Lord but also they ordered all the following [days] to be observed until the rising of the sun of the next day.

7. If, however, anyone commits a crime against another during the aforesaid truce, let him make double compensation and then let him amend

2. Fita cites three feasts dedicated to Mary in the eleventh-century Catalan liturgy: the Annunciation (March 25), the Death of Holy Mary (August 15), and the Solemnity of Holy Mary (December 8) (Fita, "Cortes y usajes," 391).

3. The feast of Saint Eulalia was celebrated on December 10; that of Saint Cugat, July 25; Saint John the Baptist, June 24; Saint Lawrence, August 10; Saint Michael the Archangel, September 24; Saint Martin of Tours, November 11.

the truce of the Lord by the judgment of cold water in the see of the Holy Cross.

8. Moreover, if anyone deliberately kills a man during this truce, it was resolved by the consent of all Christians that after making the compensation for homicide he shall be condemned to exile for all the days of his life or confined in a monastery after having assumed the monastic habit.

9. The aforesaid bishops and princes ruled that the aforesaid pact of the Lord shall be rigorously kept and observed by all accompanying them in the upcoming expedition[4] or by those remaining here in this land during the entire period of this expedition until thirty days after their return. Thus it was established that none of these persons, whether those going or remaining, shall dare to wrong any other faithful person or in any of his possessions. But if he does so, let him pay double compensation for the wrongdoing and be deprived forever of Christian communion until suitable compensation shall be made by him.

10. Moreover, the aforesaid bishops and princes thus ejected from the communion of the Church and Christianity those perverse men who capture Christians to sell them to pagans [Muslims] or act for the damage of Christianity so if anyone should come upon them, he need not consider them under the [protection of] the truce of the Lord.

II: Peace Laws of Two Urgelese Villages (April 1, 1076)[5]
Agreement of Villages of Bar and Toloriu[6]

Under the sacred name of the holy and indivisible Trinity, we all the people living in the village of Bar and in the village of Toloriu wish to bring to the knowledge of all people, both present and future, that a great discord has broken out between the count of Urgel[7] and the count of Cerdanya.[8] Therefore, fearful and anxious concerning their war so that we, as nearby inhabitants, may not be thrown into disorder and deprived of nearly everything we have, we are providing as best we can in such a way that all of us and our successors shall always be safe and free from all fears and undisturbed by the Urgelese host. And coming down to the Church Holy

---

4. The international crusade against the Muslim town of Barbastro in early 1064.
5. Font Rius, "Origenes," doc. 1, pp. 552–53.
6. Villages of the diocese of Urgel on either side of the Segre River.
7. Ermengol IV of Urgel (1066–92).
8. Guillem Ramón, Count of Cerdanya (1068–95).

Mary the Mother of God, we have come before the lord Count of Urgel, namely Ermengol, and before the Lord Bishop Bernat who had come there with many of their best men. We asked them to grant to us and to all our posterity a peace and truce so that from then on they would commit no wrong against us. And because of this peace and truce we will build this bridge of Bar[9] and we will level all the road from the post of Aristot to the river which is called Riutort.[10] Moreover, when they heard our petition and considered our promise, it was so carried out by the will of God that they freely and truly conceded to us and God in accordance with what we have asked and we, the aforementioned men of the aforementioned villages along with all other men great or small living in the village of Bar and we along with all other men great or small living in the village of Toloriu, grant and agree to the lord God and his holy mother of the see of Vich and to Count Ermengol, Bishop Bernat and all the college of canons that we and all our progeny from this hour hereafter shall make the above-written bridge of Bar over the River Segre[11] and level the above-written road between each of the aforewritten limits so that all passing through by a straight route who should wish to travel by the road and cross the bridge may do so without any offense as long as humankind inhabits the world.

III: Peace and Truce Included in the Grant of Privileges to the Inhabitants of the Castle of Olérdola Made by Count Ramón Berenguer III [November 26, 1108][12]

We also decree and command that a peace and truce be maintained by all people — by the inhabitants of this very castle and by those coming to its defense — and we place all their property under the [protection] of the truce of the Lord and the peace for all their days when they are within these boundaries [six boundary points surrounding castle] so that after they are within these boundaries, it shall not be permissible for any person to capture them, do any wrong to them, or violate this truce and peace. And if

9. This bridge, which was built in 1076, remained standing until 1985.
10. Any of a number of small streams emptying into the Segre above La Seu d'Urgel.
11. One of Catalonia's great rivers which tracks southwestward below La Seu d'Urgel toward Lerida.
12. Font Rius, *Cartas*, I, doc. 45, pp. 77–78. Olérdola is a castle of the Alt Panades built in the ninth century on an ancient Roman site.

anyone violates it and does not make compensation within thirty days, let him be distrained by my castellans until he makes double compensation.

IV: Charter of the Peace Established in the County of Cerdanya and Conflent — 1118[13]

Let it be clear to all seeing or hearing this document that I Ramon by the grace of God Count of Barcelona and Marquess of Provence and the Lord Peter Bishop of Elna,[14] with the counsel and command of the magnates and knights of the whole county of Cerdanya and Conflent, issue a peace in the aforesaid county concerning oxen and other plowing animals and all persons touching them or plowing so that no man or woman of whatever rank should dare to steal or take them in any way or for any reason whatsoever. But let he who does this, restore the oxen to the person from whom he stole them and likewise make compensation of sixty sous of the count's money to the aforementioned count [of Barcelona]. Meanwhile, let him remain under episcopal interdict until he has fully made this restitution. Therefore the aforesaid count, with the counsel of all the aforementioned, issues his money which he has confirmed with his own hand in the aforesaid county as he has also done in his other counties for so that all the time so long as he is alive, he shall not alter or diminish the metal ratio or weight of the aforesaid coinage with the stipulation that all men and women of the aforesaid county give twelve dinars per yoke of oxen, six dinars for each man, and three dinars for ploughing equipment. Indeed the aforesaid count promises to God and to all persons of the aforesaid county that after the aforesaid dinars are given to the aforesaid count, he would never again claim the aforesaid dinars from the aforesaid men but let the aforesaid law always remain undiminished and secure and it shall not be violated by any living man or woman or through a war which the count or the aforesaid prince or knights have among themselves. Indeed from the aforesaid fine of sixty sous, let the aforementioned bishop have a third.

13. *LFM*, 2: doc. 691, p. 200; Thomas N. Bisson, *Conservation of Coinage: Monetary Exploitation and Its Restraint in France, Catalonia, and Aragon, c. 1000–1225 A.D.* (Oxford: Clarendon Press, 1979), doc. 1, pp. 199–200.

14. Village of Upper Roussillon.

V: These are the Securities of Churches and Clerics, Monks and Feast Days, Merchants, and Plowmen Established by the Bishops and the Count [1131][15]

In the one-hundred-and-thirtieth year of the Incarnation after the millennium on March 10, there gathered the venerable man O(laguer) Archbishop of Tarragona and the bishops R[amón Gaufred] of Ausona and B[erenguer Dalmau] of Gerona, abbots of the land and very many magnates in the palace of Barcelona in the presence of lord Ramón Count of Barcelona and Marquess [of Provence] and his son Ramón in order to discuss the common utility of his land.

1.–2. [Shortened version of #1 and #2 from assembly of 1064].

3. Likewise, the aforesaid bishops and princes confirmed that no person in this bishopric should rob horses or their foals and ordained that all traders who travel through the land to go to market or to court and all who go to a mill to have their flour ground, along with all their possessions, beasts, and property are under the security of the peace. They also included within the same peace oxen and other plowing animals with all their plowing equipment and the man who plows with them or leads them to pastures or guards them, and the one who plants them.

4. Let no man dare burn a house or possession of another unless exactly as specified by reason of justice and with the counsel of the bishop. But if one presumes to do otherwise, let him be subject to the decree which was promulgated by the Roman Pontiff concerning this. And until he does so, let him be excommunicate and avoided by all the Faithful.

5. [#4 of 1064 assembly on peace-infraction penalties].

15. *CAVC*, I, pt. 1: 49–51; Fidel Fita y Colomé, "Cortes de Barcelona (10 Marzo, 1131): Texto inédito," *BRAH* 4(1884): 79–82.

Appendix II: Catalan Adjudication During the Period of the *Usatges* Formation

I: Judgment by Battle Between Count Ramón IV of Pallars and Theobald for Determining Control of the Castle of Orcau (1088)[16]

Judgement of the suit which was rendered between Count Ramón[17] and Countess Valencia, and Theobald concerning the castle of Orcau[18] is as follows. If Theobald can prove that the said count and countess by their free will and without coercion had issued to him the charter which he presents concerning the control of Orcau and the aforesaid count and countess cannot rebut this by a knight and their knight is then defeated, let this aforesaid castle with all its appurtenances be proclaimed to be Theobald's. If however Theobald's knight is defeated, then let Theobald similarly proclaim this castle with all its appurtenances to be the count's and countess's. If however Teobald cannot prove this, then let the said count and countess show by the oath of one knight that they had not issued this charter with free will and without coercion. And if Theobald cannot rebut this by one knight and his knight is defeated, let him proclaim the aforesaid castle with its appurtenances to be the count's and countess's. And if the count's knight is defeated, let him and the countess proclaim this castle with its appurtenances to be Theobald's. And let this be done without fraud by both parties.

---

16. *LFM*, I: doc. 68, pp. 83–84.
17. Ramón IV, Count of Pallars Jussa (1047–98).
18. Castle of Pallars Jussa.

II: A Violent Reaction to the Judgment Rendered for a Suit Between the Count of Roussillon and the Bishop of Elna (March 24, 1100)[19]

In the name of the Lord. Let it be known to all those present and future who read or hear this charter that Arnau Guillem de Sals, overcome by an illness from which he died, for the salvation of his soul and those of his parents, made a gift to God and blessed Eulalia and made her heir with a testamentary right of a third of the village of Texneres[20] with its appurtenances and the Church of Saint Genesius with all its freeholds, tithes, first fruits, and offerings. But when Count Guislabert[21] heard this, he bore it ill because he had already seized the aforesaid village in a disgraceful spirit of avariciousness, coming to the Church of Elna, he there complained very much that Bishop-Elect Ermengol wished to take the aforementioned village from him, and he [Guislabert] began a suit against him on a certain day. After many nobles and non-noblemen as well as judges gathered from different regions, although there was manly talk among them and discussion in various ways, nothing was determined. Ramón Guillem of Empuries and Perelada and judge of the region of Roussillon, at the order and request of the aforesaid Count Guislabert, taking the judgment to himself according to the Gothic law, and inviolably, the other judges not having anything against this, ruled that Count Guislabert had no right in all those things which he was claiming to have. Indeed after this judgment was rendered according to law, the aforesaid count and his son Guirard,[22] not acquiescing at all, invaded the aforesaid village, and burning down houses, cutting down trees, and even wounding men, evilly and unjustly committed many adverse and disgraceful things in the capture of Santa Eulalia de Texneres and in certain other sites of the same region. At length on the counsel of noble and prudent men, the good Count Guislabert and his son, after being rebuked for their injustice and returning to their accustomed piety and receiving seventy sous from the Bishop-Elect Ermengol for the possessions of Santa Eulalia, returned free and clear everything Arnau Guillem gave in a grant or left in his will to God and Santa Eulalia. But if any person of any sort should contrive to act against this present proclamation or confirmation, let him gain nothing. But for the mere effrontery, let him make double compensation for all the aforementioned things while

19. *Marca*, doc. 326, pp. 1219–20.
20. Village of Santa Eulalia de Roncana in Valles Oriental.
21. Guislabert, Count of Roussillon (1074–1102).
22. Guirard I, Count of Roussillon (1102–15).

this proclamation and confirmation shall remain in force forever. And let the one who attempts this incur the wrath of God, undergo judgment with Datan and Hebron and let him share the lot of Judas the traitor.

III: Feudal Disputes Between Count Arnau Mir of Pallars and His Liege Vassal (Mid-Twelfth Century)[23]

These are the disputes Count Arnau of Pallars[24] has with Ramón de Eril.[25]

Berenguer de Benevent and his fief were under the protection of the count and this very Berenguer placed himself under the authority and command of the count so that he would post a surety for Arnau and Ramón de Eril at the command of the count. And the count issued a charter so that none should commit any offense against him and Ramón de Eril captured this shield bearer, held him captive and did 995 golden florins' damage to him.

Ramón de Eril holds Fraga[26] for the Count and made a foray there and within the boundaries of Fraga captured 990 sheep from the men of the count of Pallars and the king, from whom the count holds Fraga.

Count Arnau was captured and the King of Navarre was holding him prisoner and the count placed all his patrimony and vassals under the protection of Ramón de Eril and gave the truce of his own vassals to the vassals of the count and the count gave it for his vassals to Ramon's vassals. And during this truce, they [Ramon's vassals] did 900 sous worth of damage to the count and his vassals.

Pere de Bardet is a vassal of the count and Ramón de Eril did not want him to be accepted by the count and put him under constraint and he was made a vassal of Ramón.

Ramón de Eril is a liege vassal of the count and the count and his son sought fief service from him and he did not render it.

He owes debts to the vassals of the count and has not paid them.

In Vallebona and Bonausa, he unjustly confiscated fiefs valued at 990 sous.

He sent a guarantor, R[amón] de Valsegne, to the Count so he would not take Aran[27] from him, which he [Ramón] de Valsegne] held as a pledge

23. *LFM*, 1: doc. 68, pp. 83–84.
24. Arnau II, Count of Pallars (1124–67).
25. Ramón I, Lord of Eril and holder of the castle of Saidi.
26. Municipality of Baix Cinca on both sides of the Cinca River.
27. Pyrenean valley to the west of Pallars Sobira and above Alta Ribagorza.

for 1000 sous. He took Aran from him and he did not pay the 1000 sous and the damage to the count is 990 sous.

He accepted a pledge at Lerida and Agramunt[28] which he did not repay, and Ermengaudus, Count of Urgel, gained by judgment from him that the count must not restrain him to repay it and the men of the count must not dare to go to Lerida or Agramunt.

Berivizio wounded Pere de Castellnou, liege vassal and nephew of the count and unjustly killed a certain man of Montanyana[29] named Ros.

R[amón] de San Saturnino unjustly took twenty mules and asses from Sanc de Lirio.

The vassals of R[amón] de Eril did damage to men of Val Benasc amounting to 994 sous.

The count had set up and confirmed at Casteglo a fair with Ramón de Eril's counsel, but Ramón set up another fair and forbade his own vassals and others from coming to the [count's] fair.

This is the memorandum of those hostages which Ramón de Eril sent to the count of Pallars for the posting of sureties or judgements: Ponç de Eril is hostage for 2000 sous; Arnau de Eril is hostage for 2000 sous; Roger de Eril is hostage for 2000 sous; Bertran de Eramont is hostage for 1000 sous and Guillem de Perver the elder is hostage for 1000 sous.

Guarantors for pledges for Ramón de Eril were Ponc de Eril, 1000 sous; Pere de Vilamur, 1000 sous; Alaman, 1000 sous; Guillem de Perves, 1000 sous; Bertran de Eramont, 1000 sous.

[An incomplete record of the iuditium between these two parties survives that dealt with the infractions during the peace and truce. Ramón de Eril's confiscation of property outside Fraga, his illegal activity while the count was a prisoner in Navarre, and his devastation of B. de Benevent's land].

IV: Peace Settlement Between Count Ramón Berenguer IV and Count Ponç Hug I of Empuries (March 5, 1137)[30]

In the one hundred-and-thirty-seventh year of the Incarnation of the Lord after the millennium, a spontaneous peace and amicable settlement was

28. Municipality of Urgel to the northwest of Tarrega.
29. Village of Ribagorza ceded to the Hospitallers in 1175 by Count Ramón V of Pallars-Jussa.
30. *CDACA*, 4: doc. 23, pp. 55–59.

made between the venerable Count Ramón of Barcelona and Count Ponç
Hug of Empuries[31] concerning the very many disputes, offenses, and infractions of the truce and peace and fealty on account of which they often
complained to one another. Indeed first the aforesaid Count Ponç agreed to
serve faithfully his lord Count Ramón and maintain the charter of agreement and abandonment of claims which his father Count Hug [II] of
Empuries[32] made to the church of Gerona and its bishops and canons
concerning the fief which the church of Gerona has or ought to have in
Castilion and within its boundaries. And he agreed to the same count along
with the parishioners of each sex of the church of Castilion that they shall
not prevent the provost of the church of Gerona in any way from working,
holding, or exchanging these lands whenever and wherever he wishes.
Likewise, the aforementioned Count Ponç, with a spontaneous assent and
voluntary decision, agreed with him [Ramón] that he would totally destroy, eradicate, and remove settlers from the castle of Charmez. And the
aforementioned count of Barcelona agreed to remove settlers from and to
totally destroy the castle of Rocaberti under the aforesaid voluntary decision and spontaneous assent of the count of Empuries, and that the aforesaid Count Ponç on no occasion or for no reason shall be annoyed with the
aforesaid count of Barcelona because of the destruction of the aforesaid
castles. Further that the aforesaid castles shall in no way be rebuilt by the
aforesaid Count Ponç or by any counsel or deceit of his without the
voluntary permission of the aforementioned Count Ponç. Let there be a
secure peace without deceit between Ramón de Peralta and his brother
Aimeric and the aforesaid Count Ponç. And let render homage to him
[Ponç] and draw out his coinage in Perelada and let them conserve the
coinage in Perelada[33] and let this circulate at six dinars for each libra for the
fief of the aforesaid Count Ponç. Concerning the disputes of the Viscount of
Castellnou[34] and the aforementioned Count Ponç, it was decreed that after
a pledge was redeemed, the count of Barcelona shall place such peaceful
men [arbiters] there as to make a firm peace between them. Moreover, I the
aforesaid Count Ponç agrees to maintain, observe, and fulfill all the things
written above under homage and fealty to you Count [Ramón] as my lord
and to put an end to all those things by which I harmed you in word or
deed; and attend to all this by faith without deceit.

31. Ponç Hug I, Count of Empuries (1116–54).
32. Hug II, Count of Empuries (1078–1116).
33. Town and district of lower Empuries bounded by the Fluvía River.
34. Jazpert II, Viscount of Castellnou (1119–51).

[There follows a pact by which Ramón Berenguer IV grants castles and revenues held by Ponç Hug I's father in return for his homage and fealty].

V: Judgment by Comital Curia Between Ramón Berenguer IV and Galceran de Sals (Mid-Twelfth Century)[35]

This is a judgment given legally and customarily concerning charges and defenses made by the lord count of Barcelona and Galceran de Sals. Therefore, having heard and discussed the cases of both parties, the aforesaid court judged that if the count could provide by suitable witnesses that Galceran had been derelict in his duty to him in his hosts, cavalcades, and services which the count had commanded in person or by his messenger[36] and the count could prove that he summoned the host of Lorca with his barons for the purpose of battle and Galceran knew of this, let Galceran make double compensation to him. But if he could not prove this, let Galceran clear himself through an oath by his own hand that the count in person or by his messenger did not summon him to this nor did he know that the count had summoned his barons to it. It secondly judged for all the wrong and damage which Arnau de Sals with Galceran's vassals committed to Ramón de Vilamuls at the castle of Toraies or in its sanctuary (since the aforesaid Ramón was with their common lord), Galceran should make double compensation to him and amend this dishonor to the ruler with his possessions and an oath taken by a liege vassal of this foray.[37]

Likewise it judged concerning the wrong which Arnau de Sals committed against a vassal of Santa Eulalia who the count claimed to be his and then preferred charges concerning it against Arnau de Sals and Galceran, removing from them the right of a vassal since they seemed to have done this for the dishonor of the count, that Galceran shall make compensation twice over for this dishonor to his lord, the count, and the aforesaid vassal, except that done within his rights. Likewise it judged that if the count could prove that Arnau de Sals or his vassals removed anything from this estate of the aforesaid vassals and the count could prove the aforesaid estate to be his, then Galceran shall give back and restore to him twice over anything usurped from this estate and for the unlawful seizure from the count just as

35. *LFM*, 2: doc. 511, pp. 24–25.
36. Citation from *Usatges*, art. 30.
37. Drawn from *Usatges*, art. 73.

it is contained in the law.[38] Afterwards let it be determined under whose jurisdiction the aforesaid vassal is, whether of the count's or Galceran's, and let each party show this by witnesses or by a charter.

The court judged that the new fortification which Galceran made at Pol without the permission of the count be destroyed or allowed to stand according to the count's will,[39] as is contained in the customary law. Likewise it is judged that the castle of Cornella[40] after the death of Bernat Joan without legitimate descendant must come under the control of the Count without any implement in accordance with customary law which orders that all freeholds of an exorchia holder shall come under the authority of the prince,[41] except for the rights of the heirs. And it judged that since the count had postponed litigation to Galceran concerning the aforesaid castle of Cornella before he would turn over to Guillem de Cornella who claimed it was under his jurisdiction, and before Guillem de Cornella would turn over to Ramón Vilamuls his rights in the aforesaid castle with the count's counsel and since Galceran did not want to receive justice from the count for all the wrongs which Galceran and his vassals afterwards committed against the vassals of the count on this occasion, let him make compensation for the dishonor to the count and suffer his own dishonor with an oath since just as the offense done through a deprivation of justice must in no way be compensated, thus that which was done for the delay of justice must in no way remain undone so that it may not be compensated.[42] It also judged that the count shall reimburse Galceran for all expenses and losses which Galceran and his vassals incurred in the service of the count by the command of the count and his men as far as Galceran can verify these.[43] It also judged that Bernat de Bestrecan shall make compensation for the wrong which he committed in the benefice of San Miquel de Cuxa[44] and let the abbot of San Miquel distrain according to his power Ramón de Ribes to render justice to the aforesaid Bertran de Bestrecan. It judged that Galceran shall restore to the Abbot and Provost of Comprodon all the tolls and

---

38. Reference to a passage of the *Liber Judiciorum* (VIII, 1, 4) also cited in *Usatges*, art. A1.

39. Adaptation of *Usatges*, arts. 68 and 73.

40. Castle near the Llobregat River in the modern Barcelona suburb of Cornella de Llobregat.

41. Citation from *Usatges*, art. 65.

42. Citation from *Usatges*, art. 79.

43. Citation from *Usatges*, art. 30.

44. Monastery of Conflent founded in 879. After a shortlived existence, it was refounded in 953 and in 958 came under the rule of Cluny. Along with Ripoll, San Miquel de Cuxa stood as one of Catalonia's paramount cultural centers in the twelfth century.

exactions which Arnau de Sals and Galceran's vassals exacted in the village of Romanio which are not contained in the pact which is in effect between Galceran and San Pere de Comprodon[45] (which Galceran claimed had been approved and confirmed) nor shall any similar exactions be made by Galceran or his vassals. It judged that if the Prior of Santa Maria de Besalú could prove that Galceran, his father or grandfather had given or donated the fief of Dan after Galceran's father and his grandfather had fixed the aforesaid fief with the aforementioned charter of Santa Maria, let the aforementioned Galceran destroy and remove this pact and let the aforesaid fief of Dan be restored freely and in full ownership to the authority of the prior and canons of Santa Maria de Besalú. But if he fails in this proof according to the terms of this charter, let Galceran or his vassals not have any domination or lordship in the aforesaid fief. And let the knight either leave this fief to the prior or then place it under the prior's jurisdiction. The court than judged that if the count could prove that a vassal or vassals of Galceran lessened or shorted the measures of the market of Besalú since it is a shame to the ruler and detriment of the land,[46] those who were arrested shall come under the control of the count with their property. But if the count fails in this proof that Galceran acknowledged to his vassals that the aforementioned measures shall be done away with on goods which circulated as is apparent by the decree of the comital suit, let the aforesaid vassals of Galceran clear themselves by oath, judgement of boiling water, or judicial battle that they knowingly had done no fraud or deceit there.

45. Monastery to the south of Vallespir on Riutort River near the village of Comprodon. The monastery was founded in 998 and accepted the rule of Cluny in 1078.
46. Drawn from *Usatges*, arts. 60, 61, 62.

Appendix III: Feudal Documents

I: Naming of Guarantors to Assure Completion of Castle Construction (April 28, 1061)[47]

In the first year of King Philip[48] on the fourth of the kalends of May, Ricart Altemir gave to Lord Ramón, Count of Barcelona, and Lady Almodis, Countess, the guarantors Miron Riculf for a thousand sous; Ramón Remon, for another thousand; and Ramón Sanç, for another thousand that the aforesaid Ricart shall have made at Tarrega[49] two of the finest towers a hundred palms in height and a hundred in width by the next Feast of Saint Andrew[50] and from this coming Feast of Saint Andrew to the next Feast of Saint Andrew, he shall have made at Tarrega two twin towers, each fifty palms in height and fifty in width; and the keep which must be next to the aforesaid towers and twin towers, and this shall be done without deceit to the aforesaid count and countess. And let the aforesaid towers, twin towers, and keep be exactly as they were specified in this pact which the aforesaid Ricart has just made with the aforesaid count and countess. And these three thousand sous shall be worth sixty ounces of Barcelona. And if that written above is not done by the second of the two feasts of Saint Andrew, let each of the aforesaid guarantors give to the aforesaid count and countess, the thousand sous worth twenty golden ounces of Barcelona within fifteen days after the aforesaid count and countess demand the aforesaid three thousand sous from them.

47. *LFM*, doc. 65. pp. 69–70.
48. Philip I, King of France (1060–1108).
49. Urgelese city to the southwast of Agramunt.
50. November 30.

II: Feudal Pact by Which Count Ramón of Pallars Transfers Control of the Castle of Orcau to Ramón Miron in Exchange for His Recognition of the Count's Liege Lordship (February 4, 1072)[51]

In the name of God. This is a pact made between Count Ramón of Pallars[52] and his wife Countess Valencia and Ramón Miron de Orcau. The aforesaid Ramón agrees to the aforesaid count and countess from this hour that he will maintain himself in their homage and fealty just as a vassal ought do for his better and liege lord; and that he will not take on or keep any other lord without the counsel and will of the aforesaid count and countess and that he would swear fealty and the oath of homage to them only with their permission. And the aforesaid Ramón also agrees to the aforesaid count and countess that for all time they would have and hold in this castle of Orcau and in all of its boundaries and appurtenances that lordship which his father ever had and ought to have there forever from the aforesaid count, except for control of this castle. And the aforesaid agrees to the aforesaid Ramón that neither he nor his aforesaid wife or son will not demand control of the aforesaid castle; and the aforesaid count will swear an oath to the aforesaid Ramón for his life and fief. And if they demand control of the aforesaid castle if they should do such to them which they do not wish to or cannot amend, let the count or countess or their son not give it to them; nor may the aforesaid Ramón, his wife, or son grant it away; if they should commit such an offense against them [the Count and his family] for which they [the latter] should not wish nor they [the former] cannot make amends. Likewise, the aforesaid Ramón Miron agrees that he, his wife, and their children will observe and maintain the abovesaid pact to those men or women to whom the count and countess may cede and grant the castle of Orcau in the same way as they agreed to carry out and observe it to the aforesaid count and countess. And the count and countess and their son likewise will hold and maintain the aforesaid pact just as they agreed to do so to him. And if Ramón Miron loses the demesne of Cubeas, let the count restore it to him within forty days. And the aforesaid Ramón agrees that from the next coming Easter onward that he will break feudal ties with the count and countess of Urgel unless they could not extend this any longer by the will of the aforesaid count and countess [of Pallars].

51. *LFM*, 1: doc. 65, pp. 79–80.
52. Ramón IV, Count of Pallars-Jussa (1047–98).

III: Transfer of Castle by Lord to Son of Deceased Vassal (May 15, 1086)[53]

This is a pact in commemoration of an agreement which Count Bernat of Besalú[54] made with Bernat Terron. The aforesaid Count gives to aforesiad Bernat the castle of Fenollet and commends to him all of his father's fief after his father's death. And because of this, he is his vassal who shall be faithful to him for all time and post the sureties for him which he must just as his other liege vassals do and must do for him. And Bernat after the death of his father must grant freely, faithfully, and without diminution to lord God and San Paulo de Vallsol all the village of Mauri[55] with all of its appurtenances so that he shall be a vassal for all these things to lord God and Saint Paul and the aforesaid count and his son who will be the count of Besalú and his inhabitants of San Paulo without any deceit to him or theirs.

IV: Pact Concerning Holding of Multiple Fiefs (August 26, 1086)[56]

This is a pact made between Lord Ramón, Count of Pallars and Rafart Guitard and his brothers Guillem and Theobald. Indeed, the abovewritten brothers agree to the aforementioned Count Ramón that if their brother Ficapal comes they would at once post a surety for him concerning the quarrels which the aforesaid count has with them. . . . However, in the meantime, in respect of this pact the count gives them his fief just as he had given it to their aforesaid brother, and let one of them be a liege vassal to him because of this fief and let the others be his commended vassals and serve him with horsemen and footsoldiers for the portions which fall to them from the fief. However, if the aforesaid brother comes and does not post a surety with the count or does not want to in any way, let the aforesaid Rafard be the liegemen of the aforesaid count for the fief and let him serve him in hosts, expeditions and services with horsemen and foot soldiers just as a vassal must do without deceit for his liege lord. And let the other brothers render to the aforesaid count as much as it may be rightfully judged to them from the aforesaid fief. And they agree in turn to carry out

---

53. *LFM*, 2: doc. 498, pp. 10–11.
54. Bernat II, Count of Belsalú (1066–1100).
55. Village and castle of San Pere de Fenollet in Perpignan.
56. *LFM*, 1: doc. 98, pp. 105–6.

this pact without deceit to Count Ramón. However, if the count dies, they likewise agree to carry out the pact to his son Pere[57] and if he dies, to his [the Count's] other children to whom he leaves or bequeaths his county of Pallars.

V: Notarial Formula for Fealty Oath Current in the Chancellery of Ramón Berenguer III[58]

I ——, son of the woman ——, without fraud or evil intent or any deception, with righteous faith and without deceit, swear to you Ramón Count of Barcelona and Marquess of Besalú and Cerdanya, son of the woman Matilde, and to your son to whom you may leave by word or testament your realm, that from this hour on I —— will be your vassal for your life, for the limbs which are joined to your body, for your castles or fortresses, crags and hills, cultivated or wild land, alods or fiefs which you hold today or ought to hold or you will acquire in the future with my counsel and I will not take them from you. I ——, the aforesaid vassal, nor any man or woman of mine, acting on my counsel, deceit, or assent will not take them from there nor hinder you nor contest you for them; and I will be your helper, with righteous faith and without deceit, in having, holding, and defending this against all men and women.

57. Pere Ramón, first son of Count Ramón IV, who died in 1124 at the Battle of Corbins.
58. Trenchs, "Escribanía de Ramón Berenguer III," 36.

Bibliography

PRIMARY SOURCES

MANUSCRIPTS AND EDITIONS OF THE *USATGES*

Barcelona
Archivo de la Corona de Aragón
  Cancillería Real.
    Pergaminos de Alfonso II
    Pergaminos de Ramón Berenguer I
    Pergaminos de Ramón Berenguer III
    Pergaminos de Ramón Berenguer IV
    Pergaminos de Ramón Berenguer I, III, IV
    Pergaminos de Pedro II
    Registros de Jaime I(28 regs. in 33)
  Colección de Códigos
El Escorial
Real Biblioteca de San Lorenzo de Escorial
  Ms. Z, i, 3
  Ms. Z, II, 16
  Ms. Z, iii, 14
  Ms. Z, j, 4

PUBLISHED

Antiquiores Barchinonensium leges, quos vulgas usaticos appellat cum commentariis supremorum jurisconsultorum Jacobi a monte Judaica, Jacobi et Guillermi Vallesicca et Jacobi Calicii. Barcelona: NP, 1594.
El archivo condal de Barcelona en los siglos IX–X: Estudio crítico de sus fondos. Edited by Federico Udina Martorell. Barcelona: Consejo Superior de Investigaciónes Científicas, 1951.
The Burgundian Code. Translated by Katherine Fischer Drew. Philadelphia: University of Pennsylvania Press, 1972.
Caffaro, *De Captione Almerie et Tortuose.* Edited by Antonio Ubieto Arteta. Valencia: Anubar, 1973.

Capitularia Regnum Francorum. Monumenta Germaniae Historica. Legum: sectio II. Edited by Alfred Boretius and Victor Krause. 2 vols. Hanover: Hahn, 1907.

Cartas de población y franquicia de Cataluña. Edited by José Maria Font Rius. 2 vols. in 3 parts. Madrid-Barcelona: Escuela de Estudios Medievales. Publicacciónes de la Sección de Barcelona, 1969–1983.

Cartulario de "Sant Cugat" de Valles. Edited by José Rius Serra. 3 vols. Barcelona: Sobs. de López Robert et al., 1945–47.

Colección de las cortes de los antiguos reinos de Aragón y de Valencia y el principado de Cataluña. Edited by Fidel Fita y Colomé and Bienvenido Oliver y Esteller. 27 vols. Madrid: Real Academia de Historia, 1896–1922.

Colección de documentos inéditos del Archivo General de la Corona de Aragón. Edited by Prospero de Bofarull y Moscaró. 42 vols. Barcelona: J. Eusebio Montfort, 1850–56.

Compilación del derecho civil especial de Cataluña. Ley de 21 de Julio 1960. Barcelona: Caracas Patronat de Cultura Terra Firma, 1962. Reprint Barcelona: Generalitat de Catalunya, Departament de Justicia, 1984.

Constitucions de Catalunya. Edited by Josep M. Font Rius. vol. 4/1 of *Textos juridics catalans lleis i costums.* Barcelona: Generalitat de Catalunya, Departament de Justícia, 1988.

Constitutiones de Catalunya. Barcelona: Pere Michel and Diego Gumiel, 20 Feb., 1495.

Constitutiones y altres drets de Cathalunya compilats en virtut de capitol de cort LXXXII de las corts del Rey Don Philip IV nostre senyor celebradas en la ciutat de Barcelona any MDCCII. Barcelona: Joan Pau Marti y Joseph Lllopis Estampers, 1704. Reprint Barcelona: Editorial Base, 1973

Cronica de San Juan de la Peña. Edited by Antonio Ubieto Arteta. Valencia: Anubar, 1961. Edited by Carmen Orcastegui. Zaragoza: Diputación Privincial, Institución "Fernando el Católico," 1985. Translated by Lynn H. Nelson, under the title *The Chronicle of San Juan de la Peña: A Fourteenth-Century Official History of the Crown of Aragon.* Philadelphia: University of Pennsylvania, 1991.

La documentación pontificia hasta Inocencio III, 965–1261. Edited by Demetrio Mansilla y Reoyo. *Monumenta Hispaniae Vaticana,* no. 1, Rome: Instituto Español de Estudios Eclesiásticos, 1955.

Documentos de Jaime I de Aragón. Edited by Ambrosio Huici Miranda and Maria Desamparados Cabanes Pecourt. 4 vols. Valencia: Anubar, 1976–1982.

El fuero de Jaca. Edited by Mauricio Molho. Zaragoza: Escuela de Estudios Medievales, Instituto de Estudios Pirenaicos, 1964.

El fuero latino de Teruel. Edited by Jaime Caruana Gómez de Barreda. Teruel: Instituto de Estudios Turolenses, 1974.*Gesta comitum barchinonensium. Textos llatí i català.* Edited by Louis Barrau-Dihigo and Jaume Massó Torrents. *Cròniques catalanes,* no. 2. Barcelona: Institut de Estudis Catalans, 1925.

Gudiol, Mossen Josep. "Traducció dels Usatges, les mes antiques constitucions de Catalunya y Costumes de Pere Albert." *Anuari* 1(1907): 285–334.

The History of Feudalism. Edited by David Herlihy. New York: Walker, 1970. Reprint London: Macmillan, 1971.

Isidori Hispalensis Episcopi. *Etymologiarum sive originum libri XX*. Edited by W. M. Lindsay. 3 vols. Oxford: Clarendon Press, 1911.

Laws of the Alamans and Bavarians. Translated by Theodore John Rivers. Philadelphia: University of Pennsylvania Press, 1977.

Leges Visigothorum. Monumenta Germaniae Historica. Legum: sectio I. Edited by Karl Zeumer. Hanover: Hahn, 1902.

Legis Romanae Wisigothorum fragmenta ex codice palimpsesto Sanctae Legionensis Ecclesiae. Madrid: Ricardum Fe, Regiae Academiae Typographum, 1896. Reprint León: Fundación Sanchez-Albornoz, 1991.

Liber Feudorum Maior. Edited by Francisco Miguel Rosell. 2 vols. Barcelona: Consejo Superior de Investigaciónes Científicas. Sección de Estudios Medievales de Barcelona, 1945–47.

Libri Feudorum in Vol. 2 of *Corpus Juris Civilis in Quatuor Partes Distinctum*. Edited by Dionysius Gothfred (Jacques Godefroy). 2 vols. Frankfurt-am-Main: Sumptibus Societatis imprimiebat H. Polichias, 1663. Reprint. 1726.

El "Llibre Blanch" de Santes Creus. Edited by Federico Udina Martorell. Barcelona: Consejo Superior de Investigaciónes Científicas, 1947.

The Lombard Laws. Translated by Katherine Fischer Drew. Philadelphia: University of Pennsylvania Press, 1973.

Marca hispanica sive limes hispanicus, hoc est, geographica et historica Cataloniae, Ruscinonis, et circumiacentium populorum. Compiled by Pierre de Marca; edited by Étienne Baluze. Paris: F. Maguet, 1688. Reprint Barcelona: Editorial Base, 1972.

Pandectae Justinianae in novum ordinem Digestae cum Legibus Codicis et Novellis quae Jus Pandetarum confirmant, explicant, aut abrogant. Edited by Robert Joseph Pothier. 4 vols. Paris: Apud Sugrain patrem, J. Desaint & C. Sailant, 1748–52; Paris: Dondey-Dupré, 1818.

Sacrorum conciliorum nova et amplissima collectio. Edited by Giovani Domenico Mansi et al. 52 vols. Paris: H. Welter, 1903–27. Reprint. Graz: Akademishe Drack-u Verlag-Sansalt, 1960–69.

A Source Book of Mediaeval Europe. Edited by Frederick Austin Ogg. New York: Cooper Square Publishers, 1907. Reprint 1972.

The Theodosian Code. Translated by Clyde Pharr. Princeton, NJ: Princeton University Press, 1952.

Tractatum Petri Alberti canonici barchinonensis de consuetudines Cataloniae inter dominos & vassalos ac nonnullis aliis que commemorationes Petri Alberti apellantur. Edited by Johannes de Socarrats. Barcelona: apud Johannem Gordioliam, 1551; Lyon: apud Antonium Vincentium, 1551.

Traducción al Castellano de los Usajes y demas derechos de Cataluña. Translated and Edited by Pedro Nolasco Vives y Cebria. 4 vols. Barcelona: Libreria Ne Plus Ultra, 1861. Madrid: Libreria Emilio Font, 1861. Reprint, Edited by Joan Eges i Fernandez Barcelona: Generalitat de Catalunya. Departament de Justícia, 1984.

Los Usatges de Barcelona y els Commemoracions de Pere Albert. Els Nostres Classics, 43–44. Edited by Josep Rovira i Ermengol. Barcelona: Editorial Barcino, 1933.

Los Usatges de Barcelona: Estudios, comentarios y edición bilingüe del texto. Malaga/
   Barcelona: Universidad de Malaga/Promociónes Publicaciónes Universitarías
   de Barcelona, 1984
Usatges de Barcelona. Edited by Ramon d'Abadal i Vinyals and Ferran Valls Taberner.
   Texts de Dret Català, 1. Barcelona: Deputació Provincial, 1913.
Usatges de Barcelona. El codi a mitjan segle XII. Edited by Joan Bastardas. Barcelona:
   Fundació Noguera, 1984.

SECONDARY SOURCES

Abels, Richard P. *Lordship and Military Obligation in Anglo-Saxon England*, Berke-
   ley: University of California Press, 1988.
Albert, Ricart and Joan Gassitot, eds. *Parlaments a corts catalanes*. Barcelona: Edi-
   torial Barcino, 1928.
Anderson, Perry. *Passages from Antiquity to Feudalism*. Atlantic Highlands, NJ:
   Humanities Press, 1974. Reprint. London: NLB, 1975.
Aragó, Antonio M. and José Trenchs Odena. "Las escribanías reales catalano-
   aragónesas de Ramón Berenguer IV a la minoría de Jaime I." *RABM* 80
   (1977): 421–42.
Arregui Lucea, Luis Felipe. "La curia y los cortes en Aragón." *Argensola* 4(1953): 1–
   36.
Bachrach, Bernard S. and David Nicholas, eds. *Law, Custom, and the Social Fabric in
   Medieval Europe: Essays in Honor of Bruce Lyon*. Kalamazoo, MI: Medieval
   Institute Publications, 1990.
Baer, Yitzhak. *A History of the Jews in Christian Spain*. Translated by Louis Schoff-
   man. 2 vols. Philadelphia: Jewish Publication Society, 1961. Originally pub-
   lished as *Die Juden im christlichien Spanien*. Berlin: Akademie Verlag, 1929.
Balari Jovany, José. *Origenes históricos de Cataluña*. 2 vols. Barcelona: Hijos de J.
   Jepas, 1899. Reprint Abadia de San Cugat de Valles: Instituto Internaciónal de
   Cultura Romanica, 1964.
Bastardas i Parera, Joan. *Sobre la problematica de Usatges de Barcelona*. Barcelona: Real
   Academia de Buenas Letras de Barcelona, 1977.
Baudon de Mony, Charles. *Relations politiques des comtes de Foix avec Catalogne
   jusqu'au commencement du XIVe siècle*. Paris: A. Picardet et Fils, 1896.
Baüml, Franz H. "Varieties and Consequences of Medieval Literacy and Illiteracy."
   Speculum 55(1980): 237–65.
Benson, Robert L. and Giles Constable, eds. *Renaissance and Renewal in the Twelfth
   Century*, Cambridge, MA: Harvard University Press, 1982.
Bishko, Charles Julian. "The Spanish and Portuguese Reconquest." In *History of the
   Crusades*, edited by Kenneth M. Setton et al. 6 vols. Madison: University of
   Wisconsin Press, 1962–1969. 3: 396–457.
Bisson, Thomas N. *Conservation of Coinage: Monetary Exploitation and Its Restraint
   in France, Catalonia, and Aragon, c. 1000–1225 A.D.* Oxford: Clarendon Press,
   1979.
———. "Feudalism in Twelfth-Century Catalonia." *Structures féodales*, 172–92.

———. *The Medieval Crown of Aragon: A Short History*. Oxford: Clarendon Press, 1986.

———. "The Military Origins of Medieval Representation." *AHR* 71(1966): 1198–1218.

———. "The Organized Peace in Southern France and Catalonia, ca. 1140–ca. 1230." *AHR* 82(1977): 290–303.

———. "The Problem of Feudal Monarchy: Aragon, Catalonia, and France." *Speculum* 53(1978): 466–78.

———. "Ramon de Caldes (c.1135–c.1200): Dean of Barcelona and King's Minister." *Law, Church, and Society: Essays in Honor of Stephan Kuttner*. Edited by Kenneth Pennington and Robert Somerville. Philadelphia: University of Pennsylvania Press, 1977. 281–92.

Black, Anthony. *Political Thought in Europe, 1250–1450*. Cambridge: Cambridge University Press, 1992.

Bloch, Marc Leopold Benjamin. "European Feudalism." In *Theories of Society: Foundations of Modern Sociological Theory*, edited by Talcott Parsons et al. 2 vols. New York: Free Press 1961. Reprint 1965. 2: 385–92.

———. *French Rural History: An Essay on Its Basic Characteristics*. Translated by Janet Sondheimer. Berkeley: University of California Press, 1966. Originally published as *Les caracterés originaux de l'histoire rurale française*. Cambridge, MA: Harvard University Press, 1931. Oslo: H. Aschenhaug, 1931.

Bofarull y Moscaró, Prospero. *Los condes de Barcelona vindicados y cronologia y genealogia de los reyes de España*. 2 vols. Barcelona: Imprenta de J. Oliveres y Montmany, 1836. Reprint Barcelona: La Vanguardia, 1988.

Bonnassie, Pierre. *La Catalogne du milieu du XIe à la fin du XIe siècle: croissance et mutation d'une société*. 2 vols. Toulouse: Association des Publications d'Université de Toulouse, 1975–6.

———. "Un contrat agraire inédit du monastère du Sant Cugat (28 Août, 1040)." *AEM* 3(1966): 444–50.

———. "Les conventions féodales dans la Catalogne du XIe siècle." *Les structures sociales de l'Aquitaine, du Languedoc, et de l'Espagne au premier âge féodal*. Paris: Éditions du Centre National de la Recherche Scientifique, 1969. 187–208.

———. "Du Rhône à la Galice. Genèse et modalités du régime féodal." *Structures féodales*, 17–55.

———. "A Family of the Barcelona Countryside and Its Economic Activities Around the Year 1000." In *Early Medieval Society*, edited by Sylvia Lettice Thrupp. New York: Appleton-Century-Crofts, 1967. 103–27.

———. "Sur la formation du féodalisme catalan et sa première expansion (jusqu'à 1150 environ)." *EG*, 7–21.

———. *From Slavery to Feudalism in South-Western Europe*. Translated by Jean Birrell. Cambridge: Cambridge University Press, 1991.

Bono, José. *Historia del derecho notarial español*. 2 vols. Madrid: Junta de Decanos de los Colegios Notariales de España, 1979.

Borrell Macia, Antoni. "Els Usatges, primer codi de costums d'occident." *Cristianidad* 338(April 1–15, 1959): 223–26.

Bosch, Andreu. *Summari, index, o epitome dels admirables y nobillisims lo tots de honor de Catalunya, Rosello, y Cerdanya*. Perpinyan: Pere Lacavalleria, Estamper, 1628. Reprint. Barcelona: Curial, 1974.

Botet y Sisó, J. "Los Usatges de Barcelona: Estudis històrichs y crítichs de la primer compilació de lleys catalans." *La Renaxensa* 1(1871): 17–18, 29–31, 41–43, 53–57, 73–75.

Brandt, Joseph August. *Toward the New Spain. The Spanish Revolution of 1868 and the First Republic*. Chicago: University of Cicago Press, 1933. Reprint. Philadelphia: Porcupine Press, 1976.

Broca y Montagut, Guillem Maria de. *Història del derecho de Cataluña*. Barcelona: Herederos de J. Gili, 1918. Reprint. Barcelona: Generalitat de Catalunya. Departament de Justícia, 1985.

——. "Juristes y jurisconsuls catalans del segles XI, XII, y XIII. Fonts del seus coneixements y transcendencia." *Anuari* 2(1908): 429–42.

——. "Traça de classificació del *Usatges* y idea de la *potestat*." *Anuari* 1(1907): 274–76.

——. "Els Usatges de Barcelona." *Anuari* 5(1913–14): 357–89.

Brutails, Jean-Auguste. *Études sur la condition des populations rurales du Roussillon au Moyen Âge*. Paris: Imprimérie Nationale, 1891. Reprint. Geneva: Slatkine-Megariotis Reprints, 1975.

Brynteson, William E. "Roman Law and Legislation in the Middle Ages." *Speculum* 41(1966): 420–37.

Burns, Robert Ignatius, S.J. *The Crusader Kingdom of Valencia: Reconstruction on a Thirteenth-Century Frontier*. 2 vols. Princeton, NJ: Princeton University Press, 1967.

——. "Canon Law and the Reconquista: Convergence and Symbiosis in the Kingdom of Valencia Under Jaume the Conqueror (1213–76)." *Proceedings of the Fifth International Congress of Medieval Canon Law*. Vatican City: International Congress of Medieval Canon Law, 1980. 387–424.

——. *Islam Under the Crusaders: Colonial Survival in the Thirteenth-Century Kingdom of Valencia*. Princeton, NJ: Princeton University Press, 1975.

The Cambridge History of Medieval Political Thought, c. 350–c. 1450. Edited by James Henderson Burns. Cambridge: Cambridge University Press, 1988.

Carreras i Candi, Francesch and Siegfried Bosch. "Desafiaments de Catalunya en segle XVI." *BRABLB* 16(1933–36): 39–64.

——. "La institució del castla en Cataluña." *Miscelánea histórica catalana*. 2 vols. Barcelona: Casa Provincial de Caridad, 1905–18.

Caruana Gómez de Barreda, Jaime. "Los mayordomos de Aragón en los siglos XII y XIII." *RABM* 62(1956): 350–69.

Cervantes Saavedra, Miguel de. *The Adventures of Don Quixote*. Translated by John M. Cohen. New York: Penguin Books, 1983.

Chabás y Lloréns, Roque. *Génesis del derecho foral*. Valencia: Imprenta de Francisco Vives Mora, 1902. Reprint. 1909.

Chejne, Anwar G. *Muslim Spain: Its History and Culture*. Minneapolis: University of Minnesota Press, 1974.

Cheyette, Frederick L. "The "Sale' of Carcassone to the Counts of Barcelona (1067–1070) and the Rise of the Trancavels." *Speculum* 63(1988): 826–64.

Clanchy, Michael T. *From Memory to Written Record, 1066–1301.* Cambridge, MA: Harvard University Press, 1979. Reprint Oxford: Basil Blackwell, 1993.

Collins, Roger. *The Arab Conquest of Spain, 710–797.* London: Basil Blackwell, 1989.

———. "Charles the Bald and Wilfrid the Hairy." In *Charles the Bald: Court and Kingdom,* edited by Margaret T. Gibson and Janet L. Nelson. Oxford: Oxford University Press, 1981. 169–85.

———. *Early Medieval Spain: Unity in Diversity, 400–1000.* New York: St. Martin's Press, 1983.

———. *Law, Culture, and Regionalism in Early Medieval Spain.* Aldershot: Variorum Reprints, 1992.

I Congrés d'història de la corona de Aragó, dedicat al rey en Jaume I y la seva època. 2 vols. numbered as one. Barcelona: Ayuntamiento de Barcelona, 1909–13

VII Congrés d'història de la corona d'Aragó. 3 vols. Barcelona: Ayuntamiento de Barcelona, 1963–64.

X Congrés d'història de la corona d'Aragó. Jaime I y su època. 3 vols. Zaragoza: Institución "Fernando el Catolico," 1980.

Corbella y Pascual, Arturo. "Concordancia entre el texto catalan oficial y los latinos de Amoros y Ferrer y ensayo de restitución del texto primitivo de la colección denominada Usajes de Barcelona." *Revista jurídica de Catalunya* 13(1907): 156–76.

Coroleu i Pella, José. "Código de los Usajes de Barcelona. Estudio crítico." *BRAH* 4(1884): 85–104, 389–427.

Curchin, Leonard A. *Roman Spain: Conquest and Assimilation.* London: Routledge, 1991.

d'Abadal i de Vinyals, Ramón. "Les partidas y Catalunya." *EUC* 6(1912): 13–37, 161–81.

———. *Els primers comtes catalans. HC,* vol 1. Barcelona: Editorial Vicens Vives, 1983.

———. "La vida política y sus dirigentes." *Historia de España,* edited by Ramón Menendez Pidal. 37 vols. Madrid: Espasa-Calpe, 1963–84. 16: xlv–xciv.

Diccionari biogràfic. 4 vols. Barcelona: Albertí, Editor, 1966–1970.

Dictionary of the Middle Ages. Edited by Joseph R. Strayer et al. 13 vols. New York: Scribners, 1982–89.

Donahue, Charles A. "Law, Civil—Corpus Juris, Revival and Spread." *DMA* 7: 418–25.

Dozy, Reinhart Pieter Anne. *Spanish Islam: A History of the Moslems in Spain.* Translated by Francis Griffin Stokes. London: Chatto and Windus, 1913. Reprint. London: Frank Cass, 1972.

Duby, Georges. *The Chivalrous Society.* Translated by Cynthia Postan. Berkeley: University of California Press, 1977. Reprint. 1980.

Engels, Odilo. *Shutzgedanke und Landesherrschaft Im östlichen Pyrenäenraum (9.–13. Jahrhundert).* Munich: Ashendorff Verlagsbuchhandlung, 1970.

Ficker, Julius. "Über die *Usatici Barchinonae* und deren zusammenhang mit den *Exceptiones Legum Romanorum.*" *Mitteilungen des instituts fur österreichische geschichtsforschung* 1(1886): 136–275.

Fichtenau, Heinrich. *The Carolingian Empire: The Age of Charlemagne.* Translated by Peter Munz. 1957. Reprint New York: Harper, 1964.

Fisher, William Bayne and Howard Bowen-Jones. *Spain: An Introductory Geography.* London: Chatto and Windus, 1958. Reprint New York: Praeger, 1966.

Fita y Colomé, Fidel. "Cortes de Barcelona (10 Marzo, 1131). Texto inédito." *BRAH* 4(1884): 79–83.

——. "Cortes y Usajes de Barcelona en 1064." *BRAH* 27(1890): 385–428.

——. "El obispo Guislaberto y los Usajes de Barcelona." *BRAH* 28(1891): 228–49.

Font Rius, José Maria. "La comarca de Tortosa a raiz de la reconquista cristiana (1148)." *CHE* 19(1953): 104–28.

——. "El desarrollo general del derecho en los territorios de la Corona de Aragón." VII *CHCA*, 1: 289–326.

——. "En IX centenario del primer código catalan: Los *Usatges de Barcelona.*" *Cristianidad* 338(April 1–15, 1959): 220–2.

——. "Las fuentes históricas de la compilación." *Compilación de derecho civil,* 400–406.

——. "Origenes del regimen municipal de Cataluña." *AHDE* 16(1945): 389–529; 17(1946): 229–585.

Ford, Richard. *A Hand-Book for Travellers in Spain and Readers at Home.* 3 vols. London: Murray, 1845. Reprint. Carbondale: Southern Illinois University Press, 1966.

La formació i expansió del feudalisme català. Actes del Col.loqui Organizat per Col.legi Universitari de Girona, 8–11 de Gener de 1985: Homenatge a Santiago Sobreques i Vidal. Edited by Jaume Portella i Comas. *Estudi General,* vols. 5–6. Gerona: Col.legi Universitari de Girona, 1985–86.

Forey, Alan J. *The Military Orders from the Twelfth to the Fourteenth Centuries.* Toronto: University of Toronto Press, 1992.

——. *The Templars in the Corona de Aragon.* London: Oxford University Press, 1973.

Freedman, Paul. "Catalan Lawyers and the Origins of Serfdom." *Mediaeval Studies* 4(1986): 288–314

——. *The Diocese of Vic: Tradition and Regeneration in Medieval Catalonia.* New Brunswick, NJ: Rutgers University Press, 1983.

——. "The Enserfment Process in Medieval Catalonia: Evidence from Ecclesiastical Sources." *Viator* 13(1982): 225–44.

——. *The Origins of Peasant Servitude in Medieval Catalonia.* Cambridge: Cambridge University Press, 1991.

Ganshof, François Louis. *Feudalism.* Translated by Philip Grierson. London: Longman, 1952. Reprint New York: Harper, 1961.

——. "The Last Period of Charlemagne's Reign: A Study in Decomposition." In Ganshof, *The Carolingians and the Frankish Monarchy: Studies in Carolingian History,* translated by Janet Sondheimer. Ithaca, NY: Cornell University Press, 1971.

Garcia Gallo, Alfonso, *Curso de historia del derecho español.* 2 vols. Madrid: Grafica Administriva, 1947; Madrid: A.G.E.S.A., 1971.

——. *Manual de historia del derecho español*. 2 vols. Madrid: Artes Graficas y Ediciónes, 1975. Reprint 1984.

Giordanengo, Gerard. "Vocabulaire et formulaires féodeaux en Provence et en Dauphine (XIIe–XVIe siècles)." *Structures féodales*, 85–107.

Glossarium mediae et infimae latinitatis. Edited by Charles du Fresne, Lord du Cange. 10 vols. Paris: Firmen Didot, 1837–8.

Goebel, Julius. *Felony and Misdemeanor: A Study in the History of Criminal Law*. New York: The Commonwealth Fund, 1938. Reprint Philadelphia: University of Pennsylvania Press, 1976.

Goñi Gaztambide, José. *História de la bula de la cruzada en España*. Vitoria: Editorial del Seminario, 1958.

Gouron, André. "Gênes et le droit provençal." In Gouron, *Études sur la diffusion des doctrines juridiques médiévales*. London: Variorum Reprints, 1987. 7–15.

——. "Aux origines de l'influence des glossateurs en Espagne." *Études*, 325–46.

——. "La science juridique française aux XIe et XIIe siècles: diffusion du droit de Justinien et influences canoniques jusqu'à Gratien." *Études*, 3–118.

Guterman, Simeon. *From Personal to Territorial Law: Aspects of the History and Structure of the Western Legal Constitutional Tradition*. Metuchen, NJ: Scarecrow Press, 1972.

Handbuch der Quellen und Literatur der neuren europäischen Privatrechts Geschichte. Vol. 1, *Mittelalter: Die Geleheten Rechte und die Gesetzgebung*. Edited by Helmut Coing. 3 vols. in 7 parts. Munich: Beck, 1973–88.

Haskins, Charles Homer. *The Normans in European History*. New York: Houghton Mifflin, 1915. Reprint New York: Frederick Ungar, 1959, 1966.

——. *The Renaissance of the Twelfth Century*. Cambridge, MA: Harvard University Press, 1939. Reprint New York: New American Library, 1972.

Hernández Tejero, Francisco. "Sobre el concepto de '*potestas*'." *AHDE* 17(1946): 605–24.

Hinojosa y Naveros, Eduardo de. "La admisión del derecho romano en Cataluña." *Obras completas*. 3 vols. Madrid: Ministerio de Justicia. Consejo Superior de Investigaciónes Científicas, 1948–74. 2: 389–401.

——. *El régimen señorial y la cuestion agraria en Cataluña durante la edad media*. Madrid: Libreria General de Victorian Súarez, 1905.

Hordern, Peregrine and Nicolas Purcell. *The Mediterranean World: Man and Environment in Antiquity and the Middle Ages*. Oxford, 1987.

Houston, James Macintosh. *The Western Mediterranean World. An Introduction to Its Regional Landscapes*. London: Longman, 1964. Reprint New York: Praeger, 1967.

Iglesia Ferreirós, Aquilino. "La creación del derecho en Cataluña." *AHDE* 47 (1977): 99–423.

Jolowicz, Herbert F. "Political Implications of Roman Law." *Tulane Law Review* 22(1947): 62–81.

Jones, Arnold Hugh Martin. *Augustus*. London: Chatto and Windus, 1970. Reprint. New York: W. W. Norton, 1971.

Kagay, Donald J. "Catalonia." In *Historical Dictionary of Modern Spain*, 1700–1988, edited by Robert W. Kern. New York: Greenwood Press, 1988. 125–29.

——. "Structures of Baronial Dissent and Revolt Under James I (1213–76)." *Mediaevistik* 1(1988): 61–85.

——. "Violence Management in Twelfth-Century Catalonia and Aragon." In *Marginated Groups in Spanish and Portuguese History*, edited by William D. Phillips, Jr. and Carla Rahn Phillips. Minneapolis: Society for Spanish and Portuguese Historical Studies. 1989. 11–21.

Keen, Maurice. *Chivalry*. New Haven, CT: Yale University Press, 1984.

Kennelly, Karen, C.S.J. "Catalan Peace and Truce Assemblies." *Studies in Medieval Culture* 5(1975): 41–51.

——. "Sobre la paz de Dios y sagrera en el condado de Barcelona (1030–1130)." *AEM* 5(1968): 107–36.

Kern, Fritz. *Kingship and Law in the Middle Ages*. Translated by S. B. Chrimes. Oxford: Basil Blackwell. 1939. Reprint Westport, CT: Greenwood Press, 1985.

Kienast, Walter. "La pervivencia del derecho godo en el sur de Francia y Cataluña." *BRABLB* 35(1973–74): 265–74.

King, Paul David. *Law and Society in the Visigothic Kingdom*. Cambridge: Cambridge University Press, 1972.

Kuehn, Thomas. "Laws, Schools of." *DMA* 7: 512–17.

Kuttner, Stephan. "The Revival of Jurisprudence." In *Renaissance and Renewal in the Twelfth Century*, ed. Benson and Constable, 299–323.

Lalinde Abadía, Jesús Maria. *Iniciación histórica al derecho español*. Barcelona: Ayuntamiento de Barcelona, 1970.

——. *Los fueros de Aragón*. Zaragoza: Libreria General, 1979.

——. *La jurisdicción real inferior en Cataluña ("Corts," "Veguers," "Batlles")*. Barcelona: Ayuntamiento de Barcelona, 1966. Reprint. 1970.

Lea, Henry Charles. *The Duel and the Oath*. Parts I and II of *Superstition and Force: Essays on the Wager of Battle, the Ordeal, and Torture*. Philadelphia: Henry C. Lea, 1866. Reprint. Philadelphia: University of Pennsylvania Press, 1974.

——. *The Ordeal*. Part III of *Superstition and Force*. Reprint. Philadelphia: University of Pennsylvania Press, 1974.

Levy, Ernst. "The Reception of Highly-Developed Legal Systems by People of Different Cultures." *Washington Law Review and State Bar Journal* 25(1950): 233–45.

Lewis, Archibald R. "Cataluña como frontera militar (870–1050)." *AEM* 5(1968): 15–29.

——. "Count Gerald of Aurillac and Feudalism in South Central France in the Early Tenth Century." *Traditio* 20(1969): 41–58.

——. *The Development of Southern French and Catalan Society, 718–1050*. Austin: University of Texas Press. 1965.

Livermore, Harold V. *The Origins of Spain and Portugal*. London: Allen and Unwin, 1971.

Lomax, Derek. *The Reconquest of Spain*. London: Longman, 1978.

López-Aranguren, Eduardo. "Autonomía y descentralización: Las relaciónes entre el poder central y los poderes autonómicos." *Las nacionalidades del estado español: Una problematica cultural*. Minneapolis: University of Minnesota Press, 1986. 69–83.

Lynch, John. *Spain Under the Hapsburgs*. 2 vols. Oxford: Oxford University Press, 1964. Reprint New York: New York University Press, 1981.

Maravall, José Antonio. *El Concepto de España en la Edad Media*. Madrid: Instituto de Estudios Politicos, 1964; Madrid: Centro de Estudios Constitutionales, 1981.

———. *Estudios de historia del pensamiento español*. 2 vols. Madrid: Ediciones Cultura Hispanica, 1972. Reprint 1983.

Massot-Reynier, J. *Les coutumes de Perpignan*. Montpellier: J. Martel, aine imprimieur de la Société Archéologique, 1848; Marseilles: Laffitte Reprints, 1976.

Mateu i Llopis, Felipe. "El '*aureum Valencie*' en los '*Usatici Barchinone*.' Estudio de las clausulas, fuentes pecuniarias de las Usatges." *Numisma* 6(1956): 12–27.

McKitterick, Rosamond, ed. *The Frankish Kingdom Under the Carolingians, 751–987*. London: Longman, 1983.

———. *The Carolingians and the Written Word*. Cambridge: Cambridge University Press, 1989.

———, ed. *The Uses of Literacy in Early Medieval Europe*. Cambridge: Cambridge University Press, 1990.

Miret y Sans, Joaquim. "Escolars catalans al estudi de Bolonia en la XIII al XIV centuria." *BRABLB* 8(1915): 137–55.

Mor, Carlo Guido. "En torno al la formación del texto de los '*Usatici Barchinonae*.'" *AHDE* 27–8(1957–58): 412–59.

Mundó, Anscari. "Els manuscrits de '*Liber Judicorum*' de las comarques gironines." *EG* 5–6(1985–86): 77–86.

Myers, Henry A. *Medieval Kingship: The Origins and Development of Western Monarchy in All Stages from the fall of Rome to the Fifteenth Century*. Chicago: Nelson-Hall, 1972.

Nelson, Janet L. "Literacy in Carolingian Government." In *Uses of Literacy*, ed. McKitterick, 259–96.

Nicholas, Karen S. "The Role of Feudal Relationships in the Consolidation of Power in the Principalities of the Low Countries, 1000–1300." In *Law, Custom, and the Social Fabric*, ed. Bachrach and Nicholas, 113–30.

Niermeyer, Jan Frederick. *Mediae Latinitatis lexicon minus*. Leiden: E. J. Brill, 1976.

Nörr, Knut Wolfgang. "Institutional Foundations of the New Jurisprudence." In *Renaissance and Renewal in the Twelfth Century*, ed. Benson and Constable, 324–38

———. "Vierter Abschnitt. Die Kanonistishe Literatur." *Handbuch*, 1: 365–82.

O'Callaghan, Joseph F. *A History of Medieval Spain*. Ithaca, NY: Cornell University Press, 1975.

Oliver y Esteller, Bienvenido. *Historia del derecho en Cataluña, Mallorca, y Valencia y del código de los costumbres de Tortosa*. 4 vols. Madrid: Imprenta de Miguel Ginesta, 1876.

Otto, Nicolas S. *Derecho foral*. Barcelona: Bosch, 1954.

Pennington, Kenneth. "Law Codes, 1000–1500." *DMA* 7: 425–31

———. "Petri Exceptiones." *DMA* 9: 544

Pererna i Espelt, Josep. "Les condiciones de la unio de Aragó i Catalunya en un manuscrit de Valencia Rafael Marti de Viciana." *Arxiu de Textos Catalans Antics* 2(1983): 357–61.

Pi y Maragall, Francisco. *Las nacionalidades.* Madrid: Imprenta y Libreraria de E. Martinez, 1877. Reprint Madrid: Centro de Estudios Constitucionales, 1986.

Plucknett, Theodore Frank Thomas. "The Relations Between the Roman law and the English Common Law down to the Sixteenth Century: A General Survey." *University of Toronto Journal* 3(1939–40): 24–50.

Poly, Jean-Pierre and Eric Bournazel. *The Feudal Transformation, 900–1200.* Translated by Caroline Higgitt. New York: Holmes and Meier, 1981. Originally published as *La mutation féodale, Xe–XII siècles.* Paris: Presses Universitaires de France, 1980.

Pounds, Norman J. G. *An Historical Geography of Europe, 450 B.C.–A.D. 1330.* Cambridge: Cambridge University Press, 1973.

Rashdall, Hastings. *The Universities of Europe in the Middle Ages.* Edited by Frederick Maurice Powicke and Alfred Brothers Emden. 3 vols. Oxford: Clarendon Press, 1895. Reprint 1987.

Read, Jan. *The Catalans.* London: Faber and Faber, 1978.

Reilly, Bernard F. *The Medieval Spains.* Cambridge: Cambridge University Press, 1993.

Reyerson, Kathryn L. and John Bell Henneman. "Law, French; in South." *DMA* 7: 461–68.

Reynolds, Roger E. "Law, Canon: To Gratian." *DMA* 7: 395–412.

Rius Serra, José. "El derecho visigodo en Cataluña." *Gessamelte aufsatze zur cultur geschichte Spaniens,* 8: 64–80.

Ruiz, Teofilo F. "Law, Spanish." *DMA* 7: 519–20

Rodón Binué, Eulalia. *El lenguaje técnico del feudalismo en el sigle XI en Cataluña: Contribución al este de latin medieval.* Escuela de filología: filología clásica 16. Barcelona, 1957.

Rovira i Sola, Manuel. "Notes documentales sobre alguns effectes de la presa de Barcelona per al-Mansur" *Acta Historica et Arqueologica Medievalia* 1(1980): 31–45.

Sagarra i de Siscer, Ferran de. *Sigillografia catalan: Inventari, descriptio, estudi dels segells de Catalunya.* 5 vols. Barcelona: Espampa Henrich, 1916–32.

Shackleton, Margaret Reid. *Europe: A Regional Geography.* New York: Longman Green, 1934. Reprint New York: Praeger, 1964.

Shideler, John. *A Medieval Catalan Noble Family: The Montcadas, 1000–1230.* Berkeley: University of California Press, 1984.

Smith, Clifford Thorpe. *An Historical Geography of Western Europe Before 1800.* New York: Praeger, 1967.

Sobreques i Vidal, Santiago. *Els barons de Catalunya. HC,* vol. 3. Barcelona: Editorial Teide, 1957. Reprint Barcelona: Editorial Vivcens Vives, 1980.

——. *Els grans comtes de Barcelona. HC.* vol. 2 Barcelona: Editorial Aedos, 1961. Reprint Barcelona: Editorial Vicens Vives, 1980.

Soldevila, Ferran. *Historia de Catalunya.* 3 vols. Barcelona: Editorial Alpha, 1934. Reprint 1962.

Southern, Richard W. *The Making of the Middle Ages.* New Haven, CT: Yale University Press, 1953. Reprint 1968.

Strayer, Joseph R. "Feudalism." *DMA* 5: 52–57.

Structures féodales et féodalisme dans l'Occident méditerranéen, Xe–XIIIe siècles: bilán et perspectives de recherches. Colloque International Organisé par le Centre de la Recherche Scientifique et l'École Française de Rome, Rome, October 1978. Rome: École Française de Rome, 1983.

Taylor, Lily Ross. *Party Politics in the Age of Ceasar.* Berkeley: University of California Press, 1961. Reprint 1971.

Traggia, Joaquim. "Illustración del reynado de Don Ramiro II de Aragón." *MRAH* 31(1799): 497–592.

Trenchs Odena, Josep. "La escribanía de Ramón Berenguer III (1097–1131): Datos para su estudio." *Saitabi* 31(1984): 11–36.

———. "Los escribanos de Ramon Berenguer IV: Nuevos datos." *Saitabi* 29(1979): 5–20.

———. "Notarios y escribanos de Alfonso II(1154–1196): Datos biograficos." *Saitabi* 27(1978): 5–24.

Udina Martorell, Frederic and Antoni Maria Udina i Abello. "Consideracions a l'entorn del nucli originari dels *'Usatici Barchinonae'.*" *EG*, 87–104.

Ullmann, Walter. *The Individual and Society in the Middle Ages.* Baltimore: Johns Hopkins University Press, 1966.

———. *Law and Politics in the Middle Ages: An Introduction to the Sources of Medieval Political Ideas.* Ithaca, NY: Cornell University Press, 1975.

———. "The Medieval Papal Court as International Tribunal." *Virginia Journal of International Law* 11(1971): 356–71.

Valdeavellano y Arcimus, Luis Garcia de. *Curso de historia de los instituciones españoles de los origenes al final de la edad media.* Madrid: Revista de Occidente, 1968.

Valls Taberner, Ferran. "Los abogados en Cataluña durante la edad media." *Obras selectas.* 4 vols. (Madrid, 1954–61), 2: 281–318.

———. "Un articulat inédit de Consuetuds de Barcelona." *Obras* 2: 142–47.

———. "El Cardenal Hug Candid i els *Usatges de Barcelona* — L'estatut comtal de 1064." *Obras* 2: 76–88.

———. "Carta constitucional de Ramon Berenguer I de Barcelona (vers 1060)." *Obras* 2: 55–62.

———. "Les col.lections canoniques a Catalunya durant l'epoca comtal (1072–1162)." *Obras* 2: 96–122.

———. "La cour comtale barcelonaise." *Obras* 2: 258–75.

———. "Les descobertes de Ficker sobre els *Usatges de Barcelona* i llurs afinitats amb les *'Exceptionels Legum Romanorum'.*" *Obras* 2: 37–44.

———. "El liber iudicum popularis de Homobonus de Barcelona." *Obras* 2: 235–46.

———. "Notes sobre el duel judicial." *Obras* 2: 247–57.

———. "Noves recerques sobre els Usatges de Barcelona." *EUC* 20(1936): 70–83.

———. "Els origens dels comtats de Pallars y Ribagorza." *EUC* 9(1915–16): 1–101.

———. "El problema de la formacio del *Usatges de Barcelona.*" *Obras* 2: 45–54.

———. "Els *'usualia de curialibus usibus Barchinonae'* (assaig de reconstruccio)." *Obras* 2: 63–75.

———. *Los Usatges de Barcelona.* Edited by Manuel J. Paleaz and Enrique M. Guerra Malaga/Barcelona: Universidad de Malaga/Promociones Publicaciónes Universitarías, 1984.

Van Kleffens, Eelco Nicolaas, *Hispanic Law until the End of the Middle Ages*. Edinburgh: Edinburgh University Press, 1968.

Vicens Vives, Jaume. *Approaches to the History of Spain*. Translated by Joan Connelly
Ullman. Berkeley: University of California Press, 1967.

——. *Historia de las remensas (en el siglo XV)*. Barcelona: Editorial Vicens Vives
1978.

Vilar, Pierre. *La Catalogne dans l'Espagne moderne: Recherches sur les fondements
économiques des structures nationales*. 3 vols. Paris: S.E.V.P.E.N., 1962.

Vinagradoff, Paul. *Roman Law in Medieval Europe*. Oxford: Clarendon Press, 1929.

Vodola. Elisabeth. *Excommunication in the Middle Ages*. Berkeley: University of
California Press, 1986.

Wallace-Hadrill, John Michael. *Early Germanic Kingship in England and on the
Continent*. Oxford: Clarendon Press, 1971.

Wasserstein, David. *The Rise and Fall of the Party-Kings*. Princeton, NJ: Princeton
University Press, 1985.

Watson, Alan. *The Evolution of Law*. Baltimore: John Hopkins University Press
1985.

Watt, William Montgomery and Pierre Cachia. *A History of Islamic Spain*. 1965.
Reprint. Edinburgh: Edinburgh University Press, 1977.

Wolf, Armin. "Die Gesetzgebung der Entstehenden Territorialstäaten" *Handbuch* 1:
517–800.

——. "Gesetzgebung und Kodifikationen." In *Die Renaissance der Wissenschaften im
12. Jahrhundert*, edited by Peter Weimar. Zurich: Artemis, 1981. 143–71.

Wolff, Hans Julius. *Roman Law: An Historical Introduction*. 1951. Reprint Norman:
University of Oklahoma Press, 1976.

Wood, Ian. "Administration, Law, and Culture in Merovingian Gaul." In *Uses of
Literacy*, ed. McKitterick, 63–81.

Wormald, Patrick. *"Lex Scripta and Verbum Regis*: Legislation and Germanic Kingship, from Euric to Cnut." In *Early Medieval Kingship*, Edited by Patrick H.
Sawyer and Ian N. Wood. Leeds: The Editors, 1977. 105–38.

Zimmerman, Michel. "Aux origines de la Catalogne féodale: Les serments non dates
du regne de Ramon Berenguer Ier." *EG*, 109–49.

——. "L'usage du droit wisigothique en Catalogne du IXe au XIIe siècle." *Mélanges
de la Casa de Velasquez* 9(1973): 233–70.

Zacour, Norman. *An Introduction to Medieval Institutions*. New York: St. Martin's
Press, 1976.

Glossary

adeмperamentum	revenues from common land
affidamentum	establishment of feudal ties
aguait	ambush
aliscara	formal act of submission by a rebellious vassal
apericio	vacant feudal holding
ardimentum	military strategy
assalt	armed pursuit
averamentum	verification of a fact on oath
bachalarius	wealthy peasant
bauzia	vassalic treason
calumpnia	a legal charge
captio	capture
cavalleria terre	"kinght's fee," a land measure
cechia	irrigation canal
comitor	noble of middling rank
comunia	sworn association
condirectum	construction
conductum	safe-conduct; a soldier's fee
convenientia	charter of mutual aid between lord and vassal
disemperamentum	illegal seizure by vassals of confiscated property
diffidamentum	breaking feudal ties
emperamentum	confiscation of holding of feudal tenure
encalz	vengeance through personal attack or lawsuit
eschaza	leg irons
exovar	dowry
fallimentum	vassalic default of service
fatigatio de directo	lodging of a formal legal complaint
firmamentum de directo;	posting a surety
firmare directum	
follia	criminal slander
forisfactum	crime

guarda	castle garrison
iuvamen	vassalic aid
neglectum	damage by infringement of personal rights
peioramentum	lessening of a thing's value
potestas	overlord or ruler; custody of feudal tenture
princeps	prince; sovereign
preferimentum de directo	delay of judicial proceedings
reptementum	public accusation
statica	vassalic lodging of lord
tavega	underground prison or cell
vasvassor	middle grade noble; vassal of a vassal

Index

University of Pennsylvania Press
MIDDLE AGES SERIES
Edward Peters, General Editor

F. R. P. Akehurst, trans. *The* Coutumes de Beauvaisis *of Philippe de Beaumanoir.* 1992

Peter L. Allen. *The Art of Love: Amatory Fiction from Ovid to the* Romance of the Rose. 1992

David Anderson. *Before the Knight's Tale: Imitation of Classical Epic in Boccaccio's* Teseida. 1988

Benjamin Arnold. *Count and Bishop in Medieval Germany: A Study of Regional Power, 1100–1350.* 1991

Mark C. Bartusis. *The Late Byzantine Army: Arms and Society, 1204–1453.* 1992

J. M. W. Bean. *From Lord to Patron: Lordship in Late Medieval England.* 1990

Uta-Renate Blumenthal. *The Investiture Controversy: Church and Monarchy from the Ninth to the Twelfth Century.* 1988

Daniel Bornstein, trans. *Dino Compagni's* Chronicle *of Florence.* 1986

Maureen Boulton. *The Song in the Story: Lyric Insertions in French Narrative Fiction, 1200–1400.* 1993

Betsy Bowden. *Chaucer Aloud: The Varieties of Textual Interpretation.* 1987

Charles R. Bowlus. *Franks, Moravians, and Magyars: The Struggle for the Middle Danube, 788–907.* 1994

James William Brodman. *Ransoming Captives in Crusader Spain: The Order of Merced on the Christian-Islamic Frontier.* 1986

Kevin Brownlee and Sylvia Huot, eds. *Rethinking the* Romance of the Rose: *Text, Image, Reception.* 1992

Matilda Tomaryn Bruckner. *Shaping Romance: Interpretation, Truth, and Closure in Twelfth-Century French Fictions.* 1993

Otto Brunner (Howard Kaminsky and James Van Horn Melton, eds. and trans.). Land *and Lordship: Structures of Governance in Medieval Austria.* 1992

Robert I. Burns, S.J., ed. *Emperor of Culture: Alfonso X the Learned of Castile and His Thirteenth-Century Renaissance.* 1990

David Burr. *Olivi and Franciscan Poverty: The Origins of the* Usus Pauper *Controversy.* 1989

David Burr. *Olivi's Peaceable Kingdom: A Reading of the Apocalypse Commentary.* 1993

Thomas Cable. *The English Alliterative Tradition.* 1991

Anthony K. Cassell and Victoria Kirkham, eds. and trans. *Diana's Hunt/Caccia di Diana: Boccaccio's First Fiction.* 1991

John C. Cavadini. *The Last Christology of the West: Adoptionism in Spain and Gaul, 785–820.* 1993

Brigitte Cazelles. *The Lady as Saint: A Collection of French Hagiographic Romances of the Thirteenth Century.* 1991

Karen Cherewatuk and Ulrike Wiethaus, eds. *Dear Sister: Medieval Women and the Epistolary Genre*. 1993

Anne L. Clark. *Elisabeth of Schönau: A Twelfth-Century Visionary*. 1992

Willene B. Clark and Meradith T. McMunn, eds. *Beasts and Birds of the Middle Ages: The Bestiary and Its Legacy*. 1989

Richard C. Dales. *The Scientific Achievement of the Middle Ages*. 1973

Charles T. Davis. *Dante's Italy and Other Essays*. 1984

William J. Dohar. *The Black Death and Pastoral Leadership: The Diocese of Hereford in the Fourteenth Century*. 1994

Katherine Fischer Drew, trans. *The Burgundian Code*. 1972

Katherine Fischer Drew, trans. *The Laws of the Salian Franks*. 1991

Katherine Fischer Drew, trans. *The Lombard Laws*. 1973

Nancy Edwards. *The Archaeology of Early Medieval Ireland*. 1990

Margaret J. Ehrhart. *The Judgment of the Trojan Prince Paris in Medieval Literature*. 1987

Richard K. Emmerson and Ronald B. Herzman. *The Apocalyptic Imagination in Medieval Literature*. 1992

Theodore Evergates. *Feudal Society in Medieval France: Documents from the County of Champagne*. 1993

Felipe Fernández-Armesto. *Before Columbus: Exploration and Colonization from the Mediterranean to the Atlantic, 1229–1492*. 1987

Jerold C. Frakes. *Brides and Doom: Gender, Property, and Power in Medieval Women's Epic*. 1994

R. D. Fulk. *A History of Old English Meter*. 1992

Patrick J. Geary. *Aristocracy in Provence: The Rhône Basin at the Dawn of the Carolingian Age*. 1985

Peter Heath. *Allegory and Philosophy in Avicenna (Ibn Sînâ), with a Translation of the Book of the Prophet Muḥammad's Ascent to Heaven*. 1992

J. N. Hillgarth, ed. *Christianity and Paganism, 350–750: The Conversion of Western Europe*. 1986

Richard C. Hoffmann. *Land, Liberties, and Lordship in a Late Medieval Countryside: Agrarian Structures and Change in the Duchy of Wrocław*. 1990

Robert Hollander. *Boccaccio's Last Fiction: Il Corbaccio*. 1988

Edward B. Irving, Jr. *Rereading* Beowulf. 1989

Richard A. Jackson, ed. *Texts and Ordines for the Coronation of Frankish Kings and Queens in the Middle Ages*. 1994

C. Stephen Jaeger. *The Envy of Angels: Cathedral Schools and Social Ideals in Medieval Europe, 950–1200*. 1994

C. Stephen Jaeger. *The Origins of Courtliness: Civilizing Trends and the Formation of Courtly Ideals, 939–1210*. 1985

William Chester Jordan. *The French Monarchy and the Jews: From Philip Augustus to the Last Capetians*. 1989

William Chester Jordan. *From Servitude to Freedom: Manumission in the Sénonais in the Thirteenth Century*. 1986

Donald J. Kagay, trans. *The Usatges of Barcelona: The Fundamental Law of Catalonia*. 1994

Richard Kay. *Dante's Christian Astrology.* 1994

Ellen E. Kittell. *From* Ad Hoc *to Routine: A Case Study in Medieval Bureaucracy.* 1991

Alan C. Kors and Edward Peters, eds. *Witchcraft in Europe, 1100–1700: A Documentary History.* 1972

Barbara M. Kreutz. *Before the Normans: Southern Italy in the Ninth and Tenth Centuries.* 1992

E. Ann Matter. *The Voice of My Beloved: The Song of Songs in Western Medieval Christianity.* 1990

A. J. Minnis. *Medieval Theory of Authorship.* 1988

Lawrence Nees. *A Tainted Mantle: Hercules and the Classical Tradition at the Carolingian Court.* 1991

Lynn H. Nelson, trans. *The Chronicle of San Juan de la Peña: A Fourteenth-Century Official History of the Crown of Aragon.* 1991

Joseph F. O'Callaghan. *The Cortes of Castile-León, 1188–1350.* 1989

Joseph F. O'Callaghan. *The Learned King: The Reign of Alfonso X of Castile.* 1993

Odo of Tournai (Irven M. Resnick, trans.). *Two Theological Treatises:* On Original Sin *and* A Disputation with the Jew, Leo, Concerning the Advent of Christ, the Son of God. 1994

David M. Olster. *Roman Defeat, Christian Response, and the Literary Construction of the Jew.* 1994

William D. Paden, ed. *The Voice of the Trobairitz: Perspectives on the Women Troubadours.* 1989

Edward Peters. *The Magician, the Witch, and the Law.* 1982

Edward Peters, ed. *Christian Society and the Crusades, 1198–1229: Sources in Translation, including* The Capture of Damietta *by Oliver of Paderborn.* 1971

Edward Peters, ed. *The First Crusade: The* Chronicle of Fulcher of Chartres *and Other Source Materials.* 1971

Edward Peters, ed. *Heresy and Authority in Medieval Europe.* 1980

James M. Powell. *Albertanus of Brescia: The Pursuit of Happiness in the Early Thirteenth Century.* 1992

James M. Powell. *Anatomy of a Crusade, 1213–1221.* 1986

Susan A. Rabe. *Faith, Art, and Politics at Saint-Riquier: The Symbolic Vision of Angilbert.* 1994

Jean Renart (Patricia Terry and Nancy Vine Durling, trans.). *The Romance of the Rose or Guillaume de Dole.* 1993

Michael Resler, trans. Erec *by Hartmann von Aue.* 1987

Pierre Riché (Michael Idomir Allen, trans.). *The Carolingians: A Family Who Forged Europe.* 1993

Pierre Riché (Jo Ann McNamara, trans.). *Daily Life in the World of Charlemagne.* 1978

Jonathan Riley-Smith. *The First Crusade and the Idea of Crusading.* 1986

Joel T. Rosenthal. *Patriarchy and Families of Privilege in Fifteenth-Century England.* 1991

Teofilo F. Ruiz. *Crisis and Continuity: Land and Town in Late Medieval Castile.* 1994

Steven D. Sargent, ed. and trans. *On the Threshold of Exact Science: Selected Writings of Anneliese Maier on Late Medieval Natural Philosophy.* 1982

Robin Chapman Stacey. *The Road to Judgment: From Custom to Court in Medieval Ireland and Wales.* 1994

Sarah Stanbury. *Seeing the* Gawain-*Poet: Description and the Act of Perception.* 1992

Robert D. Stevick. *The Earliest Irish and English Bookart: Visual and Poetic Forms Before A.D. 1000.* 1994

Thomas C. Stillinger. *The Song of Troilus: Lyric Authority in the Medieval Book.* 1992

Susan Mosher Stuard. *A State of Deference: Ragusa/Dubrovnik in the Medieval Centuries.* 1992

Susan Mosher Stuard, ed. *Women in Medieval History and Historiography.* 1987

Susan Mosher Stuard, ed. *Women in Medieval Society.* 1976

Jonathan Sumption. *The Hundred Years War: Trial by Battle.* 1992

Ronald E. Surtz. *The Guitar of God: Gender, Power, and Authority in the Visionary World of Mother Juana de la Cruz (1481–1534).* 1990

William H. TeBrake. *A Plague of Insurrection: Popular Politics and Peasant Revolt in Flanders, 1323–1328.* 1993

Patricia Terry, trans. *Poems of the Elder Edda.* 1990

Hugh M. Thomas. *Vassals, Heiresses, Crusaders, and Thugs: The Gentry of Angevin Yorkshire, 1154–1215.* 1993

Ralph V. Turner. *Men Raised from the Dust: Administrative Service and Upward Mobility in Angevin England.* 1988

Mary F. Wack. *Lovesickness in the Middle Ages: The* Viaticum *and Its Commentaries.* 1990

Benedicta Ward. *Miracles and the Medieval Mind: Theory, Record, and Event, 1000–1215.* 1982

Suzanne Fonay Wemple. *Women in Frankish Society: Marriage and the Cloister, 500–900.* 1981

Jan M. Ziolkowski. *Talking Animals: Medieval Latin Beast Poetry, 750–1150.* 1993

This book has been set in Linotron Galliard. Galliard was designed for Mergenthaler in 1978 by Matthew Carter. Galliard retains many of the features of a sixteenth-century typeface cut by Robert Granjon but has some modifications that give it a more contemporary look.

Printed on acid-free paper.